EXPLORING
CELTIC
IRELAND

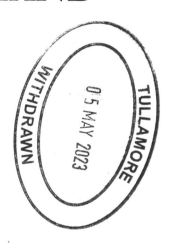

EXPLORING
CELTIC
IRELAND

PAT DARGAN

Acknowledgements

The assistance of the Dublin Institute of Technology in this production is gratefully acknowledged.

Also by the author

Exploring Georgian Dublin
Exploring Irish Castles
Exploring Ireland's Historic Towns

First published 2011

The History Press Ireland
119 Lower Baggot Street
Dublin 2
Ireland
www.thehistorypress.ie

British Library Cataloguing in Publication Data.
A catalogue record for this book is available from the British Library.

ISBN 978 1 84588 715 5

Typesetting and origination by The History Press
Printed in Great Britain

CONTENTS

GLOSSARY OF TERMS

Antae: Vertical frame-like projections at the outer edges of gable walls.

Arch: Curved head that spans an opening.

Architrave: Decorated framing around a doorway or window.

Barrel Vault: Semi-circular vaulted ceiling or roof.

Beehive Hut: Round hut, shaped like a beehive, built with corbelled stonework.

Bullaun: Small round depression carved into a large stone.

Capital: Top part of a column.

Cashel: Stone fort.

Chancel: East end of a church around the altar.

Chevaux-de-Frise: Sharp stones placed into the ground approaching a site, so as to discourage an attacking force.

Chevron: Zigzag decoration, usually in stonework.

Colonnade: Row of columns.

Column: Round stone pillar.

Corbel: Projecting stone.

Corbel Vault: Vault formed by a succession of inward corbelled stone courses, one above the other.

Crannog: A habitation site built on an artificial island.

Earthwork: A structure, usually a wall, built with earth.

Enclosure: A defined area of land, usually the internal area of a fort or monastic site.

Gable: End wall of a building.

High Cross: Tall decorated stone cross, sometimes referred to as a Celtic cross.

Inscribed Slab: Stone slab or cross with inscription.

La Tène: Abstract floral-like Celtic style of decoration.

Lintel: Flat beam spanning an opening.

Liss: Ring-fort.

Moulding: Decorative band around an opening.

Nave: Main body of a church.

Niche: Recessed opening in a wall.

Ogham: Script made up of notches cut into the edge of a stone.

Oratory: Small church.

Palisade: High fence made with wooden stakes.

Pilaster: Projecting column built into a wall.

Rath: Ring-fort.

Relief: Technique in sculpture that involves picking out an area of stone to reveal a raised decoration.

Ring-fort: Circular living enclosure formed with a bank and ditch.

Romanesque: Style of early architecture based on use of elaborately decorated round arches.

Round Tower: Tall circular bell tower.

Sacristy: Room adjoining church where robes and vessels are stored.

Shingle: Wooden roof covering like slates.

Souterrain: Man-made underground passage.

Vault: Stone archway forming the roof of chamber.

Photographs

Permission to reproduce the photographs is gratefully acknowledged from the following: Ruairi O'Neill who holds the copyright of the photograph of Lough Dhuleitie. Karl McCullagh holds the copyright of the photographs of Dun Aonghasa and Dubh Cathair. David Bayley, Studio Lab, and Irish Archaeological Consultancy Ltd who hold the copyright for the photograph of the Newtownbalregan souterrain.

ONE

CELTIC IRELAND

THE CELTS

This guide introduces the range of Celtic monuments and influences that survive across the Irish countryside today. One of the difficulties with a work such as this is that, although Ireland is very often described as a Celtic country, there is little evidence that the Celts ever came to Ireland, in any great numbers at any rate. What is known is that, from about the fourth to tenth century AD, Irish society operated under a powerful Celtic cultural influence, the physical remains of which today lie scattered all across the national landscape. These remains include ring-forts, lake dwellings, stone forts, hill forts, earthworks, monastic settlements, churches, and round towers, as well as remarkable examples of stone carvings. Before moving on to explore these remains, though, it is worth briefly reviewing what is known about the Celts, their history, their culture, and their art.

The Celts as a society originated in Western Europe and spread out across the continent in the period before the rise of Imperial Rome. During this time, they developed a highly successful Iron Age culture which was based, as the name suggests, on the use and exploitation of iron. They shared a common language, but seem to have lacked a central authority or any form of political unity. In artistic terms, the Celtic culture seems to have developed in two main phases: the Hallstatt and La Tène. Both are modern terms derived from sites near the villages of Hallstatt in Austria and La Tène in Switzerland, that produced large quantities of Celtic implements and weapons during nineteenth-century archaeological excavations. The Hallstatt phase seems to have developed between the eight and fifth century BC, when it was followed by the La Tène phase. This second phase spread across the continent and seems to have had a major artistic impact on Celtic Ireland.

The La Tène style of art is essentially organic in form and consists of floral-like abstract patterns applied to a range of surfaces, particularly wood, metal and stone. Two examples will demonstrate the characteristics of the La Tène style as it developed in Ireland. These are the decorated stone at Derrykeighan, County Antrim and the Mullaghmast Stone in the National Museum in Dublin. Figure 1 illustrates part of the Derrykeighan stone. The design here features an arrangement of curved stem-like patterns and spirals intertwined together. Figure 2 shows a similar, although more geometric pattern, on the Mullaghmast Stone. In this case, eleven circles are connected together by a system of floral, or trumpet-like, shapes.

CELTIC IRELAND

Following Caesar's conquest of Gaul in 55 BC, the Celtic civilisation went into decline across mainland Europe and was absorbed into the Roman Empire. Outside the Empire, particularly in Ireland and Scotland however, the Celtic culture survived and even advanced. In the case of Ireland, little is known about the arrival of the Celtic people. It is uncertain precisely where they came from, in what numbers they landed, or where they settled. It may be that they arrived in small numbers spread over a long period of time, rather than as a large scale invading force. Whatever the details of their arrival and settlement were, their cultural influences were enthusiastically received, although curiously, the practice of the La Tène art form seems to have been confined mainly to the northern half of the country. Other than this, scarcely anything is known about the social and political impacts of the Celtic culture on Irish life of the period. What is certain is that, by the first millennium AD

Iron Age society in Ireland operated under an all prevailing Celtic influence, and by the fourth century, the use of the Celtic language had become widespread, and went on to develop into the modern Irish Gaelic.

Apart from this, little is known about the physical and settlement patterns of the period, except for the details in a map of Europe produced by the geographer Ptolemy in about AD 200. Ptolemy's original document has failed to survive, but a record of his dimensions has allowed various researchers to reconstruct his map. The map illustrated in Figure 3, is one produced in Rome in 1490. In this example, the text is presented in Latin, rather than in the original Greek. Nevertheless, the map presents an interesting impression of Ireland at this period and identifies fifteen river estuaries, eleven towns, and the location of sixteen tribal groups. Some, but not all, of the geographical features, such as the rivers and headlands, correspond with the island's natural features of today, although the accuracy of the settlement and tribal details remain uncertain.

The fourth century AD saw the arrival of Christianity in Ireland, although it is not until four centuries or so later that any information of the social structure can be dated. This information is contained in the surviving law tracts of the period and shows that the island consisted of about 150 small kingdoms or 'tuatha'. Within these tuathas the population seems to have been divided into various levels of society. These included the king and various levels of nobles, as well as poets, artists, craftsmen, warriors, freemen, and slaves. The relationship between all of these was codified and controlled by a complex legal system often referred to as the 'Breton Laws'. Within this codified system, the freemen seem to have made up the bulk of the population. These were essentially farming family groups, who lived in a range of homesteads across the landscape that included ring-forts, stone forts, lake dwellings, and hill forts. The spread of Christianity across the country from around the fifth century onwards had a further major impact on the Irish landscape, as monastic and ecclesiastical developments made their appearance.

Today the remnants of these Celtic-influenced forts, homesteads and monastic centres survive in great numbers across the Irish landscape and act as the major focus of this guide. In terms of presentation, the contents of the guide can be seen to fit into two main historical eras. Chapters 1 to 5 introduces and explores the Celtic landscape of pre-Christian Ireland, while the Chapters 6 to 9 concentrate on the influences and impacts of Christianity. To complete the guide, Chapter 10 offers a selected list of some of the more significant Celtic sites, both secular and religious. All this is with the hope that the work will help individuals, both natives and visitors, to recognise, explore and enjoy the Celtic experiences that lie spread across the Irish countryside.

Fig. 1: Sketch, Derrykeighan Stone, County Antrim.

Fig. 2: Sketch, Mullaghmast Stone, National Museum, Dublin.

Fig. 3: Ptolemy's Map of Europe (1490), Royal Irish Academy.

TWO

RING-FORTS AND CRANNOGS

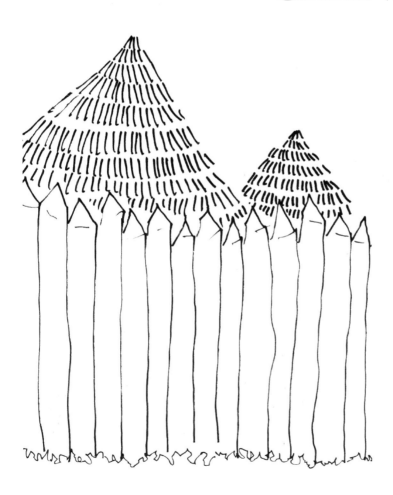

RING-FORTS

Of all the monuments on the Irish Celtic landscape, it is unquestionably the ring-fort that is the most common. Despite the name 'ring-fort' these were not defensive forts in the military sense, but the homes of farming families that provided a means of protection against the dangers of wild animals or cattle raiding. These farming activities included mainly cattle rearing, although archaeological excavations have revealed that small-scale craft and metal work was also practiced. Sometimes the ring-forts are found in loose clusters on the landscape and at other times in isolation. Traditionally ring-forts in Ireland are known by a number of different names. These include 'rath', 'liss', 'cather', 'cashel' and 'dun'. Rath and liss usually refers to smaller earth-built structures, 'Cather' and 'cashel' is the name given to stone-built forts, while 'dun' usually refers to particularly large examples. It is not without significance that all these terms can be found incorporated into local place names such as Rathgar, Lismore, Catherdaniel, and Dundalk.

In essence, the ring-fort consists of a circular or oval area surrounded by a protective bank immediately outside of which was a ditch (Fig.4). In it simplest form the ring-fort was created by digging a deep trench or ditch around the area of the fort. The spoil from the excavation was piled up inside the ditch and in this way a protective bank was created. The construction of the bank varied considerably. The bank could be topped with a wooden fence or stockade, or the bank could be faced, on both sides with wooden posts. Alternatively, where stone was plentiful, the bank could be faced with stone. All these types of construction were commonly used across the country and access to the interior of the structure was provided by a wooden gate outside of which a narrow causeway led across the ditch.

Inside the fort, a number of round or rectangular huts were erected, depending on the requirements of the occupants. These were built of wooden posts, with thatched roofs and wicker work walling. This was often made of two layers of rods woven together in a basket-like pattern, with straw, or turf, packing between the layers. This probably gave a degree of insulation to the huts. A stone hearth was placed in the centre and the beds seem to have been arranged around the walling. In terms of accommodation, two huts were sometimes joined together and these were interconnected by an internal doorway.

Fig. 4: Diagrammatic sketch, reconstructed ring-fort.

Fig. 5: Illustration of occupied ring-fort, Richard Bartley, c.1630.

The entrance to the main hut often faced east, perhaps to take advantage of the early sun. Being of wooden construction, the huts would have had a limited lifespan and as soon as a structure became unliveable, it was demolished and rebuilt, many times over, usually on, or near, the previous structure. In addition to the hut entrance, the fort gateway was also positioned on the east side. This was probably a security consideration, as it gave the occupants of the hut a clear view of the gateway.

The earliest examples of the ring-fort seem to have made their appearance during the first centuries AD and the practice continued in use until the seventeenth century. An interesting example of the late use of a ring-fort is illustrated in Richard Bartley's map of about 1630 that shows a typical ring-fort clearly occupied (Fig. 5). Numerically, it is uncertain how many ring-forts were built, as many have been destroyed in the past, especially in places where intensive agriculture has been practiced. Notwithstanding this, the number of surviving examples extends into tens of thousands and examples can be found in most areas of the country.

The size of the ring-forts varied considerably. The smaller examples usually have an internal diameter of about 15 metres, while larger examples could extend to beyond 50

Fig. 6: Base of ring-fort, Glendalough, County Wicklow.

metres. The remains of the ring-fort at Glendalough is a modest example. Here the walls were faced with stone and survive to a little below 1 metre in height (Fig.6). The larger forts had more spacious interiors and could be protected by several concentric banks and ditches with one immediately outside the other. For example, the ring-fort at Ballycrine in County Tipperary is over 30 metres in diameter and consists of a pair of concentric banks with the entrance on the south-east side (Fig.7). The banks are a mixture of stone and clay and survive to a height of around half a metre high. In addition the outline of the entrance causeway across the ditch is still identifiable. The ring-fort at Garranes in County Cork is a much larger and more complex example. Here there is a system of three banks and ditches, with an overall diameter exceeding 65 metres (Fig.8).

Given the perishable nature of wood, particularly in the Irish climate, little detailed information survives on the form of the buildings in ring-forts. One exception to this was discovered in the Deer Park Farms ring-fort in County Antrim. Here the unique ground conditions facilitated the extensive preservation of the woodwork and allowed archaeologists to undertake a detailed investigation of the internal arrangements of the structure. The original form consisted of a standard ring-fort, measuring about 20 metres across and enclosed by a single bank and ditch. However, the internal structures were demolished and rebuilt so often that the floor of the fort gradually rose to the level of the surrounding bank. Recent archaeological investigation has produced sufficient information to allow for a snapshot reconstruction of the structure as it existed around AD 700. This consisted of a pair of double circular huts, in addition to a single circular hut. The entrance to the enclosure was on the east side and was unusual in its design. This consisted of a short passage flanked on both side by the lines of the bank which were turned inwards (Fig.9).

Immediately west of the entrance was the first of the double huts. This was a circular chamber about 7 metres in diameter, immediately west of which was the second chamber, also round and measuring about 5 metres across. Both chambers were interconnected by a single doorway, giving an overall plan resembling a figure of eight. Both chambers had

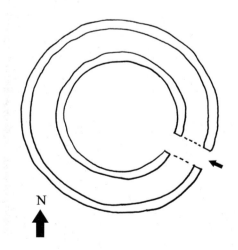

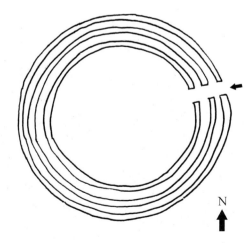

Fig. 7: Diagrammatic plan, double-bank ring-fort, Ballycrine, County Tipperary.

Fig. 8: Diagrammatic plan, three-bank ring-fort, Garranes, County Cork.

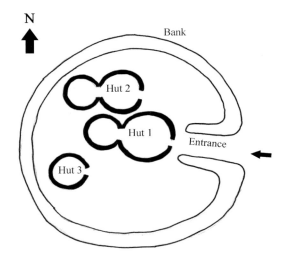

Fig. 9: Diagrammatic reconstruction, ring-fort, Deer Park Farms, County Antrim.

a central hearth while the outer one had sleeping areas around the walls. The walls themselves were made of two layers of wickerwork with grass packing between. Investigations have failed to uncover what kind of roof the structure had. The wickerwork walling may have been continued up to the central ridge and was then thatched. Alternatively, a thatched wooden framed roof may have been constructed. Immediately north of the first dwelling, a second double hut was built. This was similar in form and construction to the first, while in the south-west quarter of the enclosure a single hut was located; again with a central hearth and east facing door.

Other notable examples of ring-forts include: Ardagh in County Limerick, Aughrim in County Galway, Beal Boru in County Clare, Danestown in County Meath, Lissue in County Antrim, Lisnagade and Lisnavaragh in County Down, and Rathurles in County Tipperary. Unfortunately, most ring-forts are today in a collapsed state and often can only be identified as a low circular bank with a shallow depression running around the outside. Very often these remains are overgrown with trees and vegetation.

Fig. 10: Overgrown bank and ditch, Rathurlas ring-fort, County Tipperary.

When looking at these examples therefore, it is worth remembering that the original ditch may have been as much as 2 metres deep. The bank may have risen to a similar height and may have been topped with a wooden stockade. Over time, the stockade has rotted away and the banks have collapsed into the trench, partially filling it. All of this dramatically reduces the visual impression of the original structure. Rathurlas for example is a remarkable example with three concentric banks and ditches. While the circular interior is vegetation free, the bank system is covered with trees. Figure 10, shows a small section of the outer banks where the ditch and banks can barely be identified. Nevertheless, in most instances the internal space and the line of the enclosing bank are still recognisable, and it is possible to imagine the original form with its deep trench, the enclosing bank, wooden stockade, and internal buildings. Alternatively, an excellent example of modern reconstructed ring-fort can be seen at Ferrycarrig National Heritage Park in County Wexford (Fig.11).

CRANNOGS
In contrast to the stony ground, wetland areas offered an alternative form of housing: the lake dwelling or 'crannog' (Fig.12). The same circular or oval plan was followed, except that the structure was built on an artificial island, although occasionally natural islands played a similar role. The circular edge of the crannog was formed by large pointed logs driven into the lake bed, like piles. These were left standing well over the water line to act as stockade. The interior of the crannog was then made up by laying down successive layers

Fig.11: Reconstructed ring-fort, National Heritage Park, Ferrycarrig, County Wexford.

Fig. 12: Diagrammatic sketch of reconstructed crannog.

of brushwood, turf and gravel, although the exact flooring materials varied from site to site. As in the case of the ring-forts, a wooden gateway was incorporated into the stockade and a range of wooden huts were built for the inhabitants. Access to the mainland was by boat or by means of a narrow wooden gangway where the structure was positioned near the lake edge. Because of the cost involved in their complex construction it is probable the crannog were the homes of the more powerful or ruling families. Like the ring-forts, most crannogs date from around AD 500 and continued in use up to the seventeenth century. Another illustration by Richard Bartley from around 1630 shows an occupied crannog under attack (Fig. 13).

In numerical terms over a 1,000 crannog sites have been identified. All, as the name suggests, in lakeside or marshy locations, principally towards the central and south Ulster regions. It can, however, be difficult to identify a crannog site, as most have the appearance of small natural islands, often covered in vegetation. One exception is the recently revealed crannog in Lough Dhuleitir, Carna, County Galway. Here the reduction of the water level in the lake has exposed the base of the circular stone walls of a previously unidentified crannog (Fig. 14). Similar to the ring-fort example, excellent modern reconstructed crannogs can be seen at Ferrycarrig National Heritage Park in County Wexford (Fig. 15) and Craggaunowen in County Clare.

Fig. 13: Illustration of a crannog, Richard Bartley, *c.* 1630.

Fig. 14: Remains of crannog, Lough Dhuleitie, Carna, County Galway.

Fig. 15: Reconstructed crannog, National Heritage Park, Ferrycarrig, County Wexford.

SOUTERRAINS

Before moving on to look at the more defensive type of forts on the Celtic landscape, it is worth diverting slightly to note a feature commonly found in the interior of many ring-fort. This is the man-made underground passageway called a 'souterrain'. The purpose of these passages is uncertain, but in all probability they were used as a secure place for storing valuables, or a place of refuge in times of danger. This danger might come from an attack by a rival family, or from a party of slave raiders. The souterrain was built by excavating the required passage and chamber just below ground level. The sides were lined with stone walling and roofed over with large flat stones. The trench was then backfilled with clay and, when the vegetation grew over the backfilled area, the site was invisible. The entrance to the souterrain was sometimes located in one of the huts, or through a concealed entrance near the inner wall of the bank or stockade. A common feature of some souterrains was a built-in barrier or obstacle that acted as a measure of protection. This might take the form of a change in floor and ceiling levels, forcing attackers to crawl through a tight opening, leaving them vulnerable to attack by the defenders of the souterrain.

Like the ring-forts, the number of known souterrains runs into thousands. A small number of these have also been found in open locations, with no evidence of a relationship with an adjoining fort. In these cases, the structure of the ring-fort may have been obliterated and the souterrain forgotten about, until discovered later. Alternatively, the settlement may have consisted of an undefended cluster of huts that relied solely on the souterrain as a hiding place in the event of an attack or a raid. Fig. 16 show the souterrain at Newtownbalregan, in County Louth, being excavated. Here the roof slabs has been temporarily removed to reveal the staggered route of the passage and the stone walling. The souterrain in Drumlohan in County Tipperary is one of the few examples where the open entrance allows access to the interior of the small souterrain (Fig 17).

Many souterrains were extremely complex indeed, both in their size and in their construction. The example at Ballynee, in County Meath, for example, highlights this. Here

Fig.16: Excavated souterrain, Newtownbalregan, County Louth.

Fig. 17: Souterrain, Drumlohan, County Tipperary.

the passage seems to have been built in two stages. The first stage consists of a short straight passage that led to a single domed chamber. The entrance to the passage was on the east end and the passage ended on the far side in a dome-shaped chamber, about 3 metres wide and 2 metres high. The second stage is more complex and consisted of a 'T'-shaped passage, which crossed over the first souterrain at right angles and gave access to it (Fig. 18). The upright of the 'T' is about 15 metres long, while the cross-passage extends for about 4 metres on each side and terminated in domed chambers. These are similar in scale and form to the chamber in the first stage. The entrance to the Stage 2 passage was on the southern end of the 'T' and consisted of a narrow opening, a little over 300 millimetres high.

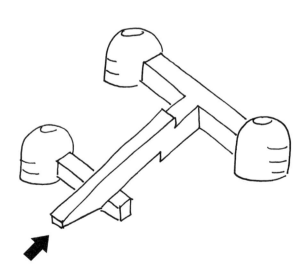

Fig. 18: Diagrammatic sketch, Ballynee Souterrain, County Meath.

THREE

STONE AND PROMONTORY FORTS

STONE FORTS

In contrast to the ring-forts, the stone built forts offer a clearer picture of their structural form and although built with stone, they are similar in scale and internal layout to the ring-forts. The only difference being that the earth and wooden structures were replaced by stone walling. Consequently, where the earthen banks of the ring-forts have collapsed, the more lasting quality of the stone walls has survived. Unlike the ring-forts, the stone fort is a more military looking structure, although like the ring-fort most seem to have served a purely domestic function. Amongst the most noteworthy of the many surviving stone forts, those at Ballykinvara, Cahercommaun and Cahermacnaughten in County Clare, Dun Aonghasa and Dun Connor on the Aran Islands, Grianan of Aileach and Dun Lough in County Donegal, Knockdrum in County Cork, and Staigue, Leacanabuaile and Cahergall in County Kerry, offer impressive examples.

Generally the stone forts are concentrated in the western area of the country, where the ground is rocky and there was a plentiful supply of suitable building stones. This is particularly true of counties Kerry, Clare and Galway where thousands of these forts survive. Like the ring-forts, they were built in both clusters and in isolation. In construction terms, the fort walling was usually constructed of two outer skins of carefully laid stonework. These facing stones seem to have been specially selected so that they could be skilfully bonded together without the use of mortar. In between the skins the internal cavity was filled with rubble to complete the walling. A special feature of some of the larger forts was the stepped terraces, or ledges, that were incorporated into the enclosure side of the wall. These step-like ledges presumably provided access to the wall top, or acted as tiered seating at special gatherings. In a number of cases, a chamber, or guard room, was incorporated into the enclosing walls and this was accessed through a small doorway from the interior of the fort. As with the ring-forts, the entrance to the stone fort usually faced eastwards and it was formed by a covered passage that ran through the walling. In addition, a number of forts were given souterrains like their ring-fort counterparts.

In regards to size, the stone forts at Staigue in County Kerry and Grianan of Aileach in County Donegal are amongst the largest and most complex examples. Of these, Staigue stands apart as one of the most impressive (Fig.19). It follows a circular plan and measures almost 30 metres across. The external wall rises nearly 6 metres high and it is about 4 metres thick. It was carefully built and incorporates an inward slope or 'batter' as it rises. The wall is faced internally with a series of terraced steps, to which access is provided by ten 'X'-shaped staircases, spaced around the wall (Fig.20). The structure was given a single entrance that ran through the wall and faced eastwards (Fig.21). The fort also has two small chambers built into the walling, with access provided by low openings inside the enclosure. Outside the fort a wide ditch was excavated and beyond this an outer earthen bank was constructed.

Grianan of Aileach is very similar in design and layout to Staigue. It measures about 24 metres wide and has a 5 metre high wall. Like Staigue, this is battered on the outside and faced internally with terraced steps. These are reached by five sets of stairs. Like Staigue, access to the interior is through a long entrance passage and there are two chambers built into the walls. The one difference between the Staigue and Grianan forts is that outside the latter three widely spaced earthen banks were completed.

Fig.19: (Above) Stone fort, Staigue, County Kerry.

Fig.20: (Left) Terraced steps, stone fort, Staigue, County Kerry.

Fig.21: (Right) Entrance, stone fort, Staigue, County Kerry.

Fig.22: Layout, stone fort, Leacanabuaile, County Kerry.

The adjacent forts of Leacanabuaile and Cahergall, in County Kerry, are smaller than Staigue, but are easier to appreciate as the interior buildings partially survive. The hilltop fort at Leacanabuaile is enclosed by an oval wall (Fig.22). The interior measures about 30 metres across and the wall is around 3 metres wide, although surprisingly it stands only a little over a metre high. The entrance faces the east and inside the enclosure the lower walls of three buildings survive (Fig. 23). The first of these is a circular hut, about 2½ metres across, which butts against the south wall of the fort. The entrance to the hut faced eastwards and just inside the doorway is the entrance to a souterrain. This follows a sharply curved line and provides access to a chamber built into the fort wall.

Some time after the construction of the circular hut, a rectangular extension measuring about 7 metres by 6, seems to have been added on the east side. The structures are interconnected while the newer chamber had an external doorway on the east side (Fig.24). The combined structure seems to have acted as the living accommodation for the family, while the two smaller structures built against the fort wall may have served as stores or animal shelters. The roofs of all these structures have vanished, but the probability is that they were built of wood and thatched. The Cahergall fort is also circular and contains

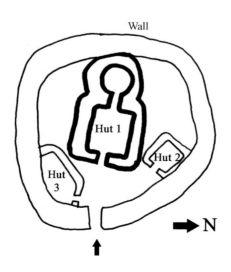

Fig.23: Stone fort, Leacanabuaile, County Kerry.

Fig.24: Interior, stone fort, Leacanabuaile, County Kerry.

Fig.25: Interior, stone fort, Cahergall, County Kerry.

the remains of an unroofed single structure (Fig.25). Like Leacanabuaile, it was built on a hilltop position, but here the walling survives to over 5 metres in height. This has internal terracing that is served by elaborate 'X'-shaped stairs (Fig 26) while the single entrance cuts through the stone walling.

Perhaps the most dramatically sited of all stone forts are those of Dun Aonghasa on Inismore, off the County Galway coast, and Cahercommaun in County Clare. The Dun Aonghasa fort is positioned with its back to the top of a 60 metre high cliff that drops sharply to the Atlantic Ocean below (Fig.27). The plan has four widely spaced walls butting against the cliff edge and arranged in a semi-circular formation one outside the other (Fig.28). The massive inner wall is around 4 metres wide and high and incorporates internal terracing, wall walks, wall chambers, and an imposing entrance that extends through the wall (Fig.29). Inside the inner wall, the 'u'-shaped interior of the fort measures roughly 50 metres from the wall face to the cliff and a little less along the cliff face.

Unfortunately the fort was heavily restored during the nineteenth century and this may have resulted in changes to the plan, particularly in the case of the outer walls, which are much lower and narrower than the inner wall. The second outer wall follows the curve of the inner wall for only half its course. Then it changes direction to enclose a large rectangular sector on the east side of the fort. This is about twice the area of the inner enclosure, although whether this was an original feature of the fort is uncertain. Outside this, the third wall only partially survives on the north side, while outside this is an extensive band of 'chevaux-de-frise' (Fig.30). This consists of range of large stake-like rocks driven into the rocky ground, so as to act as a deterrent to attackers. The width of the band varies from about 20 metres on the north side to about 10 metres on the flanking sides. This is an unusual feature, although the nearby Dubh Cathair and the Ballykinvarga fort in County Clare were both provided with similar defences. Well beyond the line of the chevaux-de-frise, the outermost wall encloses a considerable area of land. It follows a semi-circular line, but the course is irregular and a distance of around 150 metres separates it from the line of the third wall.

Equally complex is Cahercommaun Fort which, although located in an inland position, also backs onto a sheer cliff that overlooks a steep valley. In this case, a massive inner wall stands around 4 metres high by 8 metres wide and encloses a circular area with a diameter of around 32 metres. Outside this, a pair of outer walls follows a 'C' shape line from the cliff edge around the inner enclosure. An additional feature here is the four radiating walls that link the outer walling in a fan-like arrangement (Fig.31). The entrance to the inner area faces east and outside of this two of the radiating walls flank the paved entrance way. Unfortunately the walling generally is in a poor state, although archaeological excavations have shown that the inside face of the inner wall had stepped terracing like Staigue and the inner space contained a cluster of huts and two souterrains.

PROMONTORY FORTS

The use of natural defence features such as in Dun Aonghasa and Cahercommaun serve to introduce an additional type of fort: the promontory fort. In these cases natural defensive features played a major role in the location and shape of the fort. Most of these are located around the coastline although there are some inland examples. So far about 250 have been

Fig.26: Stepped interior, stone fort, Cahergall, County Kerry.

Fig.27: Dun Aonghasa stone fort, Inismore, County Galway.

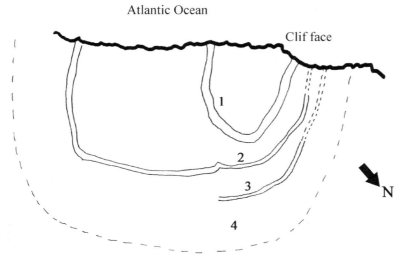

Atlantic Ocean

Clif face

1

2

3

4

N

Fig.28: Layout,
Dun Aonghasa
stone fort,
Inismore, County
Galway.
1: Inner wall
2: Middle wall
3: Outer wall
4: Chevaux-
de-frise

Fig.29: Entrance, Dun Aonghasa stone fort, Inismore, County Galway.

Fig.30: 'Chevaux–de–frise', Dun Aonghasa stone fort, Inismore, County Galway.

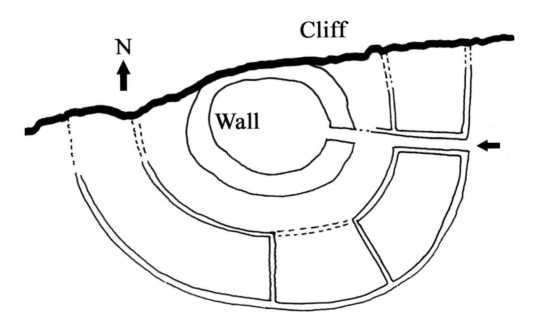

Fig.31: Caharcommaun stone fort, County Clare.

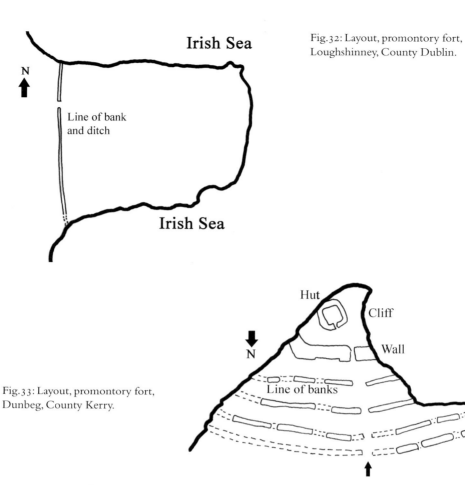

Fig.32: Layout, promontory fort, Loughshinney, County Dublin.

Irish Sea

N

Line of bank and ditch

Irish Sea

Hut

Cliff

Wall

N

Line of banks

Fig.33: Layout, promontory fort, Dunbeg, County Kerry.

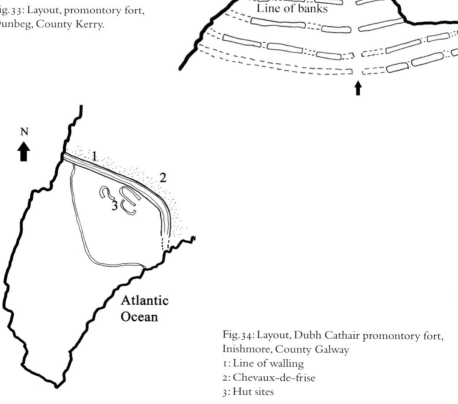

N

1

2

3

Atlantic Ocean

Fig.34: Layout, Dubh Cathair promontory fort, Inishmore, County Galway
1: Line of walling
2: Chevaux-de-frise
3: Hut sites

identified, including Loughshinny and Dalkey Island in County Dublin, Caherconree and Dunbeg in County Kerry, Dubh Cathair on the Aran Islands, and Luriegethan and Knockdhu in County Antrim. The promontory fort near Loughshinny in north County Dublin is a simple example of this type of arrangement (Fig. 32). Here the site consists of a rectangular headland of about 20 hectares that project into the Irish Sea. The site is protected on three side by side by steep cliffs, and in order to defend the site a large bank and ditch were extended across the full width on the landward side.

A much smaller, but more extensive, example is the promontory fort in Dunbeg. This is a small triangular spur of land that juts out into the Atlantic Ocean and is protected on the sea sides by steep cliffs (Fig. 33). The remains of a large circular hut, with a rectangular interior, survives at the apex of the triangle, while immediately inland of this a massive 7 metres thick stone wall stretches across from cliff edge to cliff edge. The fort has a single entrance that cuts through the wall and this is flanked on the inside by two small wall chambers. In addition to this, there is an access to a souterrain in the floor of the entrance passage. The souterrain then extends outwards well beyond the line of the wall. As if the stone wall did not offer sufficient protection, a system of four bank and five ditches were laid out on the landward side of the wall, although these have been damaged in the past. The Aughris Head promontory fort in County Sligo is similar in scale and layout to Dunbeg. In this case, the triangular spur is perched high above the Atlantic, and defended by a system of five earthen banks and ditches.

Perhaps the most spectacular example of a promontory fort is Dubh Cathair, also known as the Black Fort, on Inismore. This consists of a high almost rectangular stone platform

Fig 35: Dubh Cathair promontory fort, Inishmore, County Galway.

that juts dramatically out over the Atlantic (Fig. 34). Little, however, survives except for the massive wall that closes off the neck of the promontory. This has three stepped terraces on the inner face and a cluster of unroofed huts immediately inside the wall (Fig. 35). Access to the interior is provided by a covered entrance passage positioned about half way along the wall, while on the far side of the wall a band of 'chevaux-de-frise' guard the landward approach to the fort.

The motivation for the building of the stone and promontory forts is puzzling. Were they the homes of powerful chieftains? Did they serve a military purpose in troubled times, or were they designated ritual sites? In the case of Dun Aenghus for example, what potential enemy or attacker prompted the completion of such elaborate defence techniques? This is a puzzle that is even more intriguing in the case of the not altogether dissimilar but much larger hill forts that occupy so many upland sites.

FOUR

HILL FORTS AND EARTHWORKS

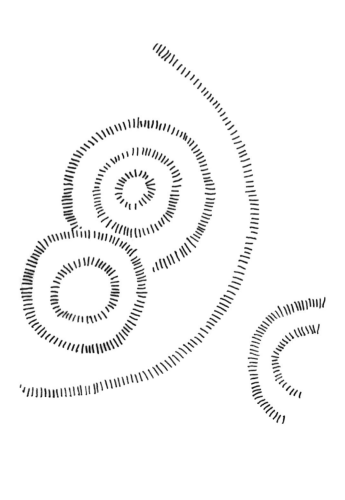

HILL FORTS

Hill forts, as the name suggests, were associated specifically with hilltop positions, where the lines of their enclosing ramparts, or banks, usually took advantage of and follow the hilltop contour lines and offered extensive views of the surrounding landscape. These were undoubtedly the largest of the Iron Age monuments to survive on the Irish landscape and they generally exceeded ten hectares or more in area. They have a structural similarity to ring-forts in that they are circular or oval in plan and are enclosed by a bank and ditch. Where they differ from the ring-fort, apart from their scale, is that the ditch is occasionally positioned inside the enclosing bank. This suggests that the structure had some non-military function, as a placing of the ditch on the inner side of a bank would make the defence awkward if not difficult. Also, most hill forts seem not to have been occupied for any long period of time and this, together with the inner ditch, suggests a community or religious function, although the hill fort as a type may have had its origins in defence.

Another common feature of many hill forts is that they occupy positions where earlier burial monuments were positioned. It may be that the earlier hilltop burial sites attracted the hill fort builders as a form of social and historic continuity. Alternatively, the choice of such sites may have been influenced solely by the strategic hilltop points they offered. The origins of most hill forts can be dated to between 300 BC and AD 500 and seem to have gone into disuse somewhere around AD 1000. In all, over eighty hill forts have been identified on the Irish landscape — mostly located in mountainous areas. Among those, Cashel Fort in County Cork, Freestone Hill in County Kilkenny, Haughey's Fort in County Armagh, Mooghaun in County Clare, as well as the Rathgall and the County Wicklow complex, offer excellent examples. The later has a most complex arrangement indeed where five hill forts are clustered together. These include Spinans Hill, Brusselstown Ring, Rathnagee, Rathcoran, Tinoranhill, and Hughstown.

When visiting a hill fort site it is worth remembering that, just like the ring-forts, the surviving banks and ditches represent only a shadow of the original structure. The banks have in many cases decayed, the ditches are partially filled in and whatever wooden stockades or buildings that existed have now vanished. Coupled with this, the sheer size of some hill forts makes it difficult to appreciate the structures in their entirety. For example Dun Aillinne in County Kildare has the appearance of a natural hill when viewed from a distance (Fig. 36). It is only when viewed from the air that the overall scale and impression of many hill forts can be appreciated.

Freestone Hill is one of the smaller hill forts and consists of a circular inner and outer enclosure (Fig. 37). The outer enclosure, which is more oval than circular, measures about 140 metres at its widest point, and covers an area of about two hectares. The bank is made from earth and rubble faced with stone. There are a number of gaps in the bank today, but the original entrance seems to have been on the west side. Outside the bank the ditch was excavated to a depth of about 2 metres. The inner enclosure is at the crown of the hill and consists of a stone-built circular wall, about 35 metres across. This is now in poor condition, although the turned-in entrance on the south-west side can still be identified. A pre-Iron Age burial cairn initially existed inside the inner enclosure, but this was seems to have been raided in the past to provide material for the enclosure walling.

Fig.36: Dun Aillinne Hill Fort, County Kildare.

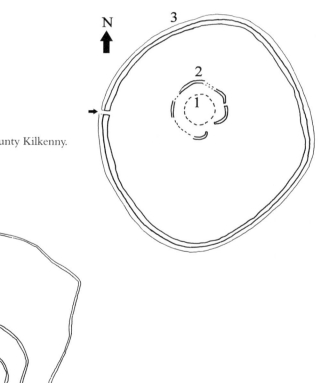

Fig.37: Plan, Freestone Hill Fort, County Kilkenny.
1: Pre-iron age burial cairn
2: Remains of inner bank
3: Outer bank and external ditch

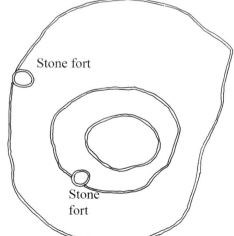

Fig.38: Plan, hill fort, Mooghaun, County Clare.

The Mooghaun hillfort in County Clare is much larger and covers an area of about eighteen hectares. It comprises three enclosures one within the other (Fig. 38). The inner enclosure is around 100 metres in diameter, while the outer enclosure reaches 400 metres at its widest. The fort also incorporates two smaller stone forts. One abuts the inside of the outer enclosure, while the other is incorporated into the line of the second enclosure bank. All three banks were built of a mixture of stone and clay, although today these are mostly overgrown.

COUNTY WICKLOW COMPLEX

The Wicklow hill fort complex is made up of six adjacent hill fort sites: Rathnagree, Rathcoran Spinans Hill, Brusselstown, Tinoranhill and Hughstown, all clustered around a bend in the River Slaney, just north of Baltinglass. The Rathcoran fort sits on the crown of Baltinglass Hill. It has a pair of oval enclosing banks and covers an area of about ten hectares (Fig. 39), with a pre-Iron Age burial complex on the crown of the hill. This is surrounded by a stone wall, but this may be of recent origins. Well downhill of the burial site, the innermost bank of the fort was built of stone. It is over 6 metres wide and survives to a height of 4 metres, immediately outside of which is a wide ditch (Fig. 40). The outer bank lies a little beyond the inner bank. It is similar in construction, but seems to have lacked a ditch. There is a short section of a third bank on the east side of the fort, although it is uncertain whether this is part of an uncompleted outer bank or an extra defence feature.

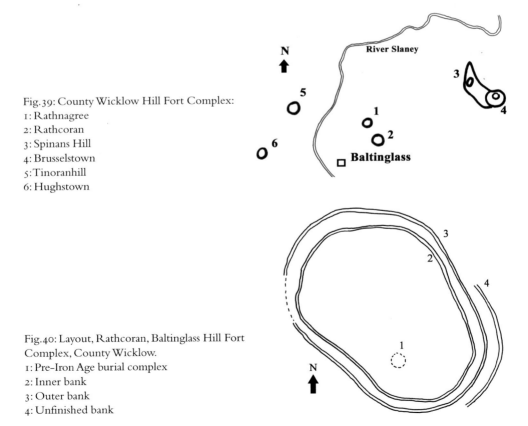

Fig. 39: County Wicklow Hill Fort Complex:
1: Rathnagree
2: Rathcoran
3: Spinans Hill
4: Brusselstown
5: Tinoranhill
6: Hughstown

Fig. 40: Layout, Rathcoran, Baltinglass Hill Fort Complex, County Wicklow.
1: Pre-Iron Age burial complex
2: Inner bank
3: Outer bank
4: Unfinished bank

The dual Spinans Hill and Brusselstown Ring site is by far the largest of the Irish hill forts. Here the site consists of a vast 'L'-shaped outer enclosure that surrounds two independent inner enclosures. (Fig.41). The higher of the two, Spinans Hill, is oval in plan and consists of a single enclosure measuring around 550 metres at its widest. The enclosing bank seems to be of earthen construction. It sits low on the landscape and can be difficult to identify. In addition, there are six earlier Neolithic burial cairns visible within the enclosure. The Brusselstown Ring lies downhill and about three quarters of a kilometre south-eastwards. It is also oval in plan and enclosed by an inner and outer enclosure. The inner enclosure is around 300 metres at it widest and it is enclosed by a substantial stone wall. This stands about 2 metres high and varies in width from 5 to 12 metres, although it is in poor shape in places. Inside the enclosure, a number of hut sites can be identified. The outer enclosure consists of a substantial double bank, unevenly spaced, but well outside the inner bank line. This was constructed with earth and stones with a ditch between. Later this bank was extended around the complete top of the mountain, where it also acted as an outer enclosure to the Spinans Hill fort. This gave the overall hill fort an area of around 130 hectares, one of the most extensive in the country.

NAVAN FORT

In a number of cases, hill forts can be linked to ceremonial or ritual practices. These include Navan Fort in County Armagh, Dun Aillinne in County Kildare and Tara in County Meath. Navan Fort, or 'Emain Macha', was the royal capital of Ulster and is one of the most puzzling of the Irish Iron Age monuments. Archaeological investigations have revealed that this was originally a Bronze Age site that consisted of a hilltop cluster of huts and other elements positioned inside a figure-of-eight enclosure. This initial complex was removed in about 100 BC and in its place was built a most remarkable structure. This was a circular wooden framework made from 275 upright posts laid out on the crown of the hill. The posts were erected around a metre and half apart so as to form a series of concentric rings, with each ring spaced about 3 metres apart. In the case of the outermost ring, the posts were spaced a little further apart and these were sheeted in horizontal wooden planks. In addition, a large individual post was erected in the centre of the complex. It is uncertain whether the structure was roofed over, or consisted solely of the uprights posts, like a wooden equivalent of the Stonehenge type of monument. Some time shortly after the completion of this structure, the entire complex was deliberately destroyed. This was completed in a most extraordinary way. First the interior of the wooden structure was filled to a height of over 2 metres with stones. Then the outer section of the wooden structure was set on fire. Following this, what remained was covered over with earth to create the flat-topped mound that is still visible on the site. Why the structure was constructed and deliberately destroyed in this way remains a mystery, but the scale of the works involved suggest that it was co-ordinated community effort.

DUN AILLINNE

Another puzzling event took place at Dun Aillinne, or the Hill of Knockaulin, in County Kildare. This has been identified as the traditional royal seat of Leinster and like Navan Fort seems to have had its origins in the pre-Iron Age period. Today the site consists of a 14-hectare oval hilltop, enclosed by a 5 metre high bank with an internal ditch (Fig.42). Recent archaeological excavations have revealed that, as was the case in Navan Fort, the

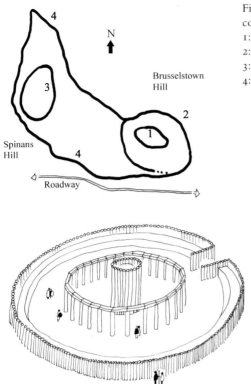

Fig.41: Brusselstown Ring/Spinans Hill, hill fort complex, County Wicklow.
1: Brusselstown inner bank.
2: Brusselstown outer bank.
3: Spinans Hill inner bank.
4: Spinans Hill outer bank.

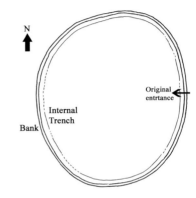

Fig.42: Layout, Dun Aillinne Hill Fort, County Kildare.

Fig.43: Conjectural restoration, Dun Aillinne Hill Fort, County Kildare.

Fig.44: Layout, Tara, County Meath.
1: Mound of the Hostages.
2: Banquet Hall.
3: Sloping Trench, North.
4: Sloping Trench, South.
5: Grainne's Fort.
6: Royal Seat.
7: Fort of the Synods.
8: Fort of the Kings.
9: Cormaic's House.
10: Laoghaire's Fort.
11: Nineteenth-century church.

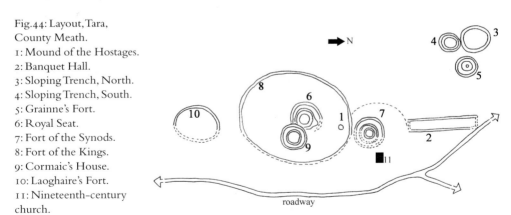

initial development was superseded by a series of later structures, which were completed in a sequence of stages. Each of these was laid over the previous one, over a time scale that extended roughly between the fifth century BC and the first century AD.

The first structure consisted of circular area enclosed by a wooden palisade, possible with terraced seating arranged against the inside of the palisade: the whole arrangement like an amphitheatre. This type of arrangement offers the possibility that the large stone forts such as Staigue and Cahergall may have served a more ceremonial than military function. Some time after its completion the structure was replaced by a second and completely different type of wooden structure. This consisted of a circular area enclosed by a palisade, which seemed to have had terraced seating built against the inner face. Inside the enclosure two further structures were built. At the centre a tall circular platform was built and around this a ring of upright posts were erected (Fig.43). Sometime later the entire structure was deliberately burnt and removed, after which the site was covered with a low mound. As is the case with Navan Fort, the ideas behind the construction and deliberate destruction of the structures is unclear. What is clearly demonstrated is that, around 100 BC, Ireland held a population of a size, and social order that allowed it to conceive and carry out large scale construction and deconstruction undertakings.

TARA

Of all the hill forts, Tara, the traditional seat of the High Kings of Ireland, is unquestionably the most famous and most complex. Unfortunately many visitors find it disappointing. The reason for this is it that the scale of the site is so large, it can be difficult to view it

Fig.45: Mound of the Hostages, Tara, County Meath.

Fig.46: Banqueting Hall, Tara, County Meath.

as a singe unit. The same also applies to the monuments themselves as the visitor can be confused by the large scale of the enclosing lines and banks. Nevertheless Tara remains one of the most significant and most easily accessible of Ireland's Iron Age sites. Taken as a whole, the site is made up of six major elements, all of which were given romantic names in the nineteenth century, which have no basis in fact. These include: the Mound of the Hostages, the Banquet Hall, the Sloping Trenches, Grainne's Fort, the Royal Seat, the Fort of the Synods, the Fort of the Kings, Cormaic's House, and the Fort of Laoghaire (Fig 44).

The earliest monuments in the Tara complex seem to be the Mound of the Hostages and the Banqueting Hall. The Mound of the Hostages is a low mound near the centre of the complex (Fig.45). This was a burial chamber that has been dated to around 2000 BC. Apart from its intrinsic significance, the mound highlights the use of the Tara Hill as a ceremonial centre well before the Iron Age period. Near the northern limit of the site, the long line of double banks was given the name the Banqueting Hall. This name was applied in the mistaken belief that the banks were the walls of the Great Banqueting Hall of Tara. In reality, the double bank structure was the formal approach to the hill fort. This approach avenue extended for about 200 metres and was flanked on both by a high bank (Fig.46). How the banks, or the overall structure, looked when completed is not known. What is known is that the monument was built between the fifth and the eight century AD — a construction date which indicates that the site at Tara was not completed in a single operation, but over a prolonged period of time.

The North and South Sloping Trenches as well as Grainne's Fort consist of a trio of circular burial enclosures clustered together, about 100 metres west of the Banqueting Hall. These seem to have been burial or ceremonial site from an earlier period. The Trenches are perched on the down slope of the hill (Fig.47) while immediately adjoining these, Grainne's Fort has a double bank and ditches, with a small burial mound in the centre. The

Fig.47: Sloping Trenches, Tara, County Meath.

Royal Seat is also an early structure. It is positioned near the centre of the Tara site and has two banks and two ditches, with a bulge in the outer bank that incorporated an earlier burial mound (Fig.48). In the centre of the enclosure is the 'Lia Fail', Stone of Destiny. This was where the kings of Tara are said to have placed their foot while being crowned.

Directly south of the Banqueting Hall is the Fort of the Synods (Fig.49). This name was applied in the belief that the Early Irish Church held a number of synods here. The present

Fig.48: Royal Seat, Tara, County Meath.

Fig.49: Fort of the Synods, Tara, County Meath.

Fig. 50: Cormaic's House, Tara, County Meath.

structure consists of a circular enclosure made up of three banks and ditches. The enclosure measures around 80 metres across and seems to be aligned on an axis with the Banqueting Hall. Unfortunately the site was badly damaged during the nineteenth century when group called the 'British Israelites' were searching for the Ark of the Covenant, which they believed lay buried there.

The Fort of the Kings is the main hill fort element of the Tara complex and consists of a large oval enclosure, positioned near the crest of the hill, with the Royal Seat and Cormaic's House near its centre. The oval-shaped interior measures around 300 metres at its widest point and it is enclosed by an earthen bank with a ditch outside, and possibly a smaller bank outside that again. Cormaic's House is a small ring-fort that buts against the east side of the Royal Seat, and consists of a small ring-fort enclosed by a double bank and ditch (Fig. 50).

At the southern end of the Tara Hill site, Laoghaire's Fort is a large circular ring-fort located about 50 metres south of Fort of the Kings. The enclosure, which extends about 125 metres across, is much damaged on he east side, with the double bank and ditch partially visible on the west side. In addition to these, over twenty-five other smaller elements lie spread out across the site, often visible only as low bumps and hollows.

LINEAR EARTHWORKS

In addition to stone and hill forts, there is another group of Iron Age monuments that can be found on the Irish landscape: the linear earthworks. These are the long lines of earthen banks or ramparts that, on occasions, wind for considerable distances across areas of the countryside and seem to have fulfilled some sort of defensive function. Amongst these are: the Doon of Drumsna in County Roscommon, the Black Pig's Dyke in south Ulster, the Black Ditch in Counties Cork and Waterford, and the Red Ditch in Counties Kerry and Limerick. In the case of Drumsna, the linear bank stretches across the neck of a natural promontory, which was formed by a double bend in the River Shannon. The bank seems

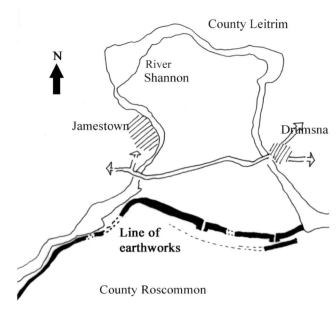

County Leitrim

N

River
Shannon

Jamestown

Drumsna

Line of
earthworks

County Roscommon

Fig. 51: Layout, Doon of Drumsna,
County Roscommon.

to have been built around 300 BC and also extends south-westwards along the river's edge for some distance. The bank itself is around 6 metres high, with an almost sheer side facing the river and a gentle slope on the Roscommon side. There is also a smaller double bank about 4 metres forward of the main bank. Today the area is overgrown with natural vegetation and tracing the course of the bank can be difficult.

The purpose of the earthwork seems to have been to present a defendable barrier to raiders who might have come from the County Leitrim side of the river. The difficulty for the defenders during this period was that there were a number of points along the loop of the Shannon that could easily be forded by a raiding or attacking force. The solution was to build the bank across the neck of the promontory to keep the raiders out (Fig. 51). However, some traffic was allowed to pass, as there were two formal gateways incorporated into the bank. These were formed by leaving a gap in the bank and extending the line of the bank southwards, so as to form a short chamber. Following this, a wooden gate was placed at either end of the chamber. If the raiders succeeded in breaching the outer gate, they would be stopped at the inner gate. At this point, the defenders could attack the raiders from the top of the bank. Who these raiders were, or where they came from, is not known. Certainly the threat was sufficient to prompt the inhabitants of the Roscommon side of the river to construct this massive defence, in addition to which recent archaeological investigation has revealed evidence of wooden chevaux-de-frise between the bank and the river's edge.

In terms of scale, the most extensive of the linear earthworks is the system collectively known as the Black Pig's Dyke, although individual sections of the Dyke have been given local names such as the Dorsey and the Dane's Cast. The course of the dyke seems to have started in south County Donegal. It then followed a gradually curved eastwards route passing through counties, Fermanagh, Leitrim, Cavan, and Monaghan (Fig. 52), to end in south County Armagh. The line of the bank itself does not form a continuous boundary. Instead it is made up of isolated sections that stretch between natural barriers such as lakes, marshes and rivers. For example, one stretch runs between Lough Melvin and Lough MacNean in County Leitrim. In many places the line of the Dyke was positioned on south-facing slopes, presumably to help deter any raiders coming from the south. The ditch itself consists usually

Fig. 52: Black Pig's Dyke, County Monaghan.

of a high earthen bank, with a ditch on one or both sides although one section in County Monaghan consisted of a double bank and ditch, and was originally topped by a wooden palisade. (Fig 52). The most extensive section of the Dyke, known as the Dorsey, spans the open land between the River Dorsey and Ummercam River. Here the Dyke was built in two stages. The first stage consisted of a curved line that joined the two rivers. For some reason this section was not considered sufficient and the second line was later laid out about 300 metres to the south. This second section was provided with a formal control point or gateway.

As was the case with Dun Aonghasa, the scale of the Black Pig's Dyke prompts the question: who built the structure and why? Certainly it was a well organised community effort that worked to some preconceived plan. It seems improbable that it had a military defence function, like Hadrian's Wall in Scotland, as the troops required to garrison it would have been considerable. On the other hand, cattle raiding seems to have been common in Iron Age Ireland, which suggests that the Dyke was built to discourage such raiding. In addition, the Dyke does not seem to have been built in a single operation, and it may be that it was completed so as to close off breaks in the natural land barriers over time. This is clear from recent archaeological evidence that dates the completed section of the Dyke in County Monaghan to between 400 BC and 100 BC, while the initial line of the Dorsey was laid out about 150 BC: to be followed around fifty years later by the second line.

The stone forts, promontory forts, hill forts and linear earthworks represent the largest and most impressive Iron Age elements on the Irish landscape. There is however one further, though infinitely smaller element, that made its appearance on the Irish landscape, particularly in the period before the arrival of Christianity in around the fourth century. These are the remarkable decorated stones whose distribution is curiously confined mainly in the northern half of the country.

FIVE

STONE CARVING

STONE CARVING

The surviving examples of Irish pre-Christian stone carving are small in number, but can nevertheless be classified into three main types. These include human figures, cult figures and decorated stones. The full human form is poorly represented amongst the surviving examples and only three examples are currently known. These include the 'Boa Island' figure and the 'Lustymore' figure, which stand beside one another on Boa Island on Lough Erne, in County Fermanagh. The Boa Island figure is the larger of the two and consists of a single stone, representing a pair of individuals standing back to back (Fig.53). The figure is just under a metre high and is currently mounted on a concrete base. Both heads are large and have a pronounced triangular shape, with large lozenge-shaped eyes and mouths. Both also have their arms extending across the front of their bodies. The figure, as it stands, is complete only from the waist up, but the lower half of the figure, with both sets of arms wrapping around the sides has recently been identified on the same site. The second example, the Lustymore figure, derives its name from the nearby island of Lusty More, from where the figure originally came. It is very similar in style to the Boa Island figure, although slightly shorter in height (Fig.54). The cathedral in Armagh also has a human-like figure named the Sun God (Fig.55) displayed in the nave. This is very small indeed and represents a human-like figure about one third of a metre high, with radiating lines extending outwards from the head. It has been suggested that the radiating lines represent the rays of the sun and this prompted the choice of the name.

Fig.53: Boa Island figure, Boa Island, County Fermanagh.

Fig.55: Sun God, Armagh Cathedral, County Armagh.

Fig.54: Lustymore figure, Boa Island, County Fermanagh.

Fig. 56: Corleck Head, National Museum of Ireland, Dublin.

Fig. 57: Cavan Head, National Museum of Ireland, Dublin.

Elsewhere, Iron Age human features are represented by heads, of which about thirty are known. Most of these heads can be found on the landscape where they were discovered or have been placed in museums. The most accomplished of the heads is unquestionably the 'Corleck Head', now displayed in the National Museum in Dublin (Fig. 56). This is an oval granite piece about one third of a metre high, with three faces distributed around the surface of the stone. Each of the faces is slightly different with circular eyes and a narrow mouth. The museum also has another example: the Cavan Head (Fig. 57). This is more oval-shaped and smaller than the Corleck Head and has a single face. The facial character is similar, with round eyes, although the mouth is more clearly defined. The 'Beltany' head, in Beltany County Donegal, is less accomplished in the execution of the facial features. The eyes are large and almond shaped, the mouth is oval with pronounced lips and the figure has large ears or some form of lugs. The face of the Armagh Head currently on display in the Church of Ireland cathedral in Armagh is similar to the Corleck head, although the features include a pronounced brushed back hair style and what looks like a beard.

CULT FIGURES

Armagh Cathedral also contains a range of cult figures which are currently displayed in the nave. These include the Tandragee Idol and the Bear Figures. The idol is a squat aggressive-looking figure consisting of a head and shoulders (Fig. 58). The large head rises straight from the body with no neck and the forehead has two projecting stubs, or horns. The left hand hangs vertically down with open fingers, while the right hand crosses the body and grasps the upper left arm. In addition, the cathedral has a pair of animal carvings. These are around 150 millimetres high and seem to represent a squatting bear or similar animal (Fig. 59). Two further, but lesser known cult figures are known to survive in private hands. These are known as the 'Armagh' and 'Lurgan' figures and are similar in form to the Tandragee figure.

Fig. 58: (Left) Tandragee Idol, Armagh Cathedral, County Armagh.

Fig. 59: (Above) Bear figures, Armagh Cathedral, County Armagh.

DECORATED STONES

In addition to figure sculptures, a number of elaborately decorated Iron Age ceremonial stones also exist in places around the landscape. These include the Turoe, Castlestrange and Killycluggin stones. As is the case with the other stone figures, their purpose is unknown, but the probability is that they fulfilled some kind of cult function. The Turoe Stone is one of the outstanding examples of La Tène stone carving within in the Celtic world (Fig.60). It stands in the grounds of Turoe House just north of Loughrea in County Galway and consists of a granite dome-topped pillar stone, almost 2 metres high. The domed section is decorated in a complex geometric pattern including interlaced, trumpet-like curves, spirals, and slender stems, all carved in relief. That is, the design was marked out on the stone and the area around was carefully chipped away until the design stood proud of the surrounding stone face. Recent studies have demonstrated that the carving is graphically arranged into four distinct panels: two D-shaped and two triangular. Each of the panels is positioned opposite its counterpart on the far side of the boulder, yet the entire reads as a single composition. The area immediately below the pattern is defined by a narrow double box-like band cut into the stone, below which the remainder of the stone is undecorated. Disappointingly, the stone is housed in a wooden hut and can only be viewed through small windows.

Fig.60: Turoe Stone, Loughrea, County Galway.

Fig.61: Castlestrange Stone, Castlestrange, County Roscommon.

The Castlestrange Stone has a number of similarities to the Turoe example. It is located about 7 kilometres south-west of Roscommon town. It is carved from granite and is entirely dome-shaped in form (Fig.61). The carving extends over most of the granite surface, although the design is cut into the stone face rather than in relief. The pattern of the carving consists of an interconnected arrangement of trumpets, curves, spirals, and stems — similar to the Turoe example, but more loosely arranged. Fortunately, it is set within a stone cobbled patio and is well presented.

The Killycluggin Stone in County Cavan was broken up at some time in the past and was only gradually reassembled. The pieces were placed in the National Museum and a full size replica of the stone now stands near its original site, about 5 kilometres south-west of Ballyconnell (Fig.62). The granite stone is dome shaped and it has been suggested that it originally formed the upper portion of a pillar stone like Turoe. The curved and spiral style of the decoration relate stylistically to the Turoe and Castlestrange stones, although the spirals are tighter. In addition, the spirals are spaced further apart and are linked by extended stems.

There are two other carved stones that differ from the Turoe, Castlestrange and Killycluggin examples, in material and form. These are the Derrykeighan and the Mullaghmast stones. The limestone Mullaghmast Stone was

Fig.62: The Killycluggin Stone, County Cavan.

found near Ballitore in County Kildare and is presently in the National Museum in Dublin. The stone is damaged at the top and base, but still partially retains its form, with oval, circular and spiral decorations on each of the faces. The principal sub-rectangular face of the stone has a sequence of eleven small circles cut into the stone in a uniform pattern and linked together with curved stems (Fig.2). The two faces of the stone above and below the main design are decorated independently. The top section has an unclear triangular pattern, while the lower panel has an intricate lozenge shaped design. The Derrykeighan Stone was found built into the wall of a church in Derrykeighan, County Antrim and is also limestone and rectangular in shape. The decoration is cut into the stone and consists of a complex geometric pattern of seven spirals linked by curved stems (Fig.1). Unfortunately, the stone has been damaged and it is difficult to indentify the top and lower ends of the pattern.

Collectively, the Celtic inspired stone work offers three intriguing questions. Who carried out the carving, why and where? The answer to these questions remains a mystery. The likelihood is that carvings had some religious or cult significance. Curiously the distribution of these figures seems to have been confined to the northern part of the country, where perhaps a specific cult or religious practices prevailed. Equally uncertain is the period when the stone workings were undertaken, although a time scale prior to the arrival of Christianity in the fourth or fifth century is most likely – following which the arrival of Christianity introduced totally new ideas in art and architecture.

SIX

EARLY CHRISTIAN BUILDINGS

CHRISTIANITY

The arrival of Christianity in Ireland during the fourth or fifth century unleashed a new force that prompted a change in society and began the second era in the development of Celtic art and architecture, a movement occasionally referred to as the Celtic Church. The introduction and spread of Christianity has traditionally been credited to St Patrick in the fifth century. There is, however, evidence that Christianity had reached the country even earlier than this, though exactly when and where remains uncertain. Whatever the case, Christianity took root and by the seventh century an extensive network of monastic foundations, both male and female, had been established all over the country, in a historical phase known as the Early Christian Period. These early Christian communities did not belong to the European monastic orders, such as the Cistercian or Augustinians, but were small religious groups that usually operated independently, although some communities shared links to a common founder, such as St Brendan. Within these early monasteries, the monks and nuns built a range of structures to cater for their spiritual and domestic requirements. These included huts, oratories, churches, cathedrals, and round towers.

BEEHIVE HUTS

The most common structures built by the monks were undoubtedly the huts where they lived. These were most probably circular in plan, built with wood and roofed with thatch. The difficulty with wood construction, however, is that it is perishable, particularly in the damp Irish climate. For this reason all traces of these wooden buildings have long since disappeared. Where wood was scarce, such as the rocky ground of western areas, the monks were forced to turn to stone as a building material, although the shape and forms of the stone structures, were influenced by that of the wooden buildings. In these cases, beehive shaped huts were constructed. These were circular structures built from large flat stones. The walls were constructed by laying layers of flat stones in a circular plan and arranged, so as to form a domed roof. This was achieved by laying each successive layer, or course, of stones so that it projected inwards over the course underneath. In this way, the inward-sloping walls of the dome was created until the structure was completed with a final single cap stone. This type of construction can clearly be seen in the number of partially demolished beehive huts on Skellig Michael, County Kerry (Fig.63). Here the walls survive to around a metre high and the gradual inward slope of the courses can be noted. In effect, the walls and roof of a beehive hut formed a continuous inward inclined curve from base to top. The result was a domed hut that was usually small and circular in plan, sufficient to accommodate a single monk (Fig.64).

Internally natural light was limited to that provided by a small single doorway. The wall of the structure was wide and laid so that the stones had a slight outward slope, that gave the structure a level of waterproofing. The corbelling technique itself was not invented by the monks, but had been in use in Ireland since the Neolithic period. For example, the same corbelling technique was used in the construction of the burial chamber in the passage tomb at Newgrange in County Meath and elsewhere. Today a large number of these beehived huts survive, particularly at Skellig Michael in County Kerry where six examples can be seen standing tucked together side by side (Fig.65).

Fig.63: Base of
beehive hut, Skellig
Michael, County
Kerry.

Fig.64: Beehive
hut, Skellig
Michael, County
Kerry.

Fig.65: Cluster of beehive huts, Skellig Michael, County Kerry.

BOAT-SHAPED ORATORIES

The beehive hut provided adequate accommodation as a monk's cell, although the circular plan was unsuitable for a church. The monks therefore adapted the corbel technique to enclose a rectangular space to form a church or oratory. By extending the circular plan lengthways a more rectangular interior space was created. The small oratory on Skellig Michael offers an example of how this was achieved. Here, the little church consisted of a single chamber or nave, around 2 metres long and 2 metres wide. It has a small narrow door on the west side and a small window low down on the opposite elevation. The walls and roof were built on the corbel system and this resulted in the building having the appearance of an up-turned boat: hence the name boat-shaped oratory.

A particularly good example of a boat-shaped church is the Oratory of Gallarus in mainland Kerry. Here the nave measures 5 metres long and 3 metres wide. It has a small door on the west side as well as a small window on the opposite wall. There was, however, a structural problem with the boat-shaped structures. This related to the characteristic of the corbelled vault. This type of structure operates successfully in the case of a circular plan, but when that plan is extended to form a rectangle, it develops a structural weakness, as there is a tendency for the vault to collapse inwards. One way to overcome this was to insert a series of wooden beams across the width of the corbelled vault. These acted as props that kept the corbelled vault from collapsing inwards. This was effective for a period, but when the wood decayed, the support was removed and the vault tended to collapse. This was the case in Gallarus (Figs.66-67) and other structures, although Gallarus has since been reconstructed.

In time, a more successful way to overcome the tendency of the corbelled vault to collapse inwards was achieved. This consisted of inserting a semi-circular vault under the corbelling: a process that resulted in creation of a small room or croft between the top corbelled vault and the lower semi-circular vault. St Columb's House in Kells is an example where this technique was successfully executed. Here the building measures nearly 6 metres long and 3 metres wide (Fig.68). In addition to creating the double arch roof structure, the builders also incorporated vertical side walls. This had the effect of defining the eaves line, from where the roof slopes upwards (Fig.69). This resulted in a building type with separately defined walls and roof (Fig.70). In its original form the building had three storeys: the basement, the ground floor nave and an overhead croft. Today ground level around the building has been lowered and the entrance is through a modern doorway cut through the basement wall on the south side of the building. The original western entrance door is now blocked up and the original wooden ground floor

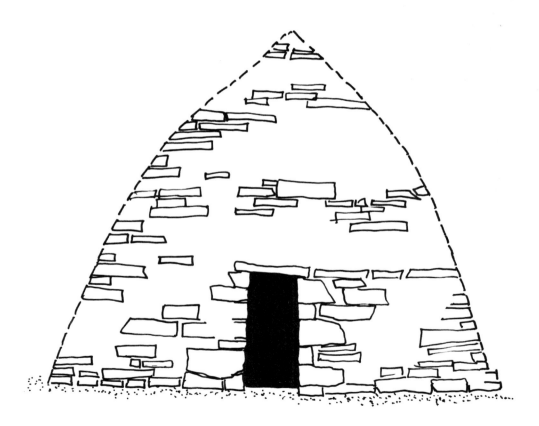

Fig.66: Gallarus Oratory, County Kerry.

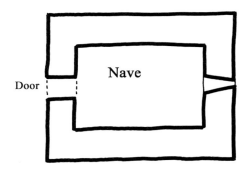

Fig.67: Plan, Gallarus Oratory, County Kerry.

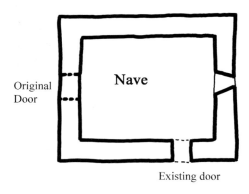

Fig.68: Plan, St Columb's House, Kells, County Meath.

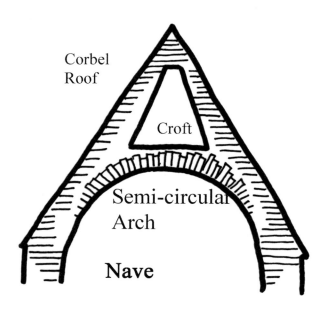

Fig.69: Roof structure, St Columb's House, Kells, County Meath.

Fig. 70: St Columb's House, Kells, County Meath.

no longer exists. The steeply sloped stone roof is built on the corbel principal, beneath which the semi-circular propping arch spans the width of the structure. This prevented the corbel arch from collapsing inwards and at the same time provided a small room, or croft, between arches. Despite the advance in the corbel construction technique, the interior of the structure is very dark, as the windows are little more than slits.

St Kevin's church in Glendalough is a similar design, but consists of a more complex and accomplished corbelled structure. Here the rectangular plan is slightly larger than St Columb's House, and has a small chancel and sacristy at the eastern end. The structure is still largely intact, although the chancel building was demolished in the past (Fig.71). The roof of the nave and surviving sacristy are both corbelled in a manner similar to St Columb's, but the structure includes a tall circular tower rising from the roof on the western end (Fig.72). Here again, a limited amount of natural light is supplied by a number of small slit-like windows. Unlike St Columb's, the western door of the nave survives. This consists of a narrow opening with a slight incline towards the top. This is spanned by a heavy beam or lintel, over which is a plain semi-circular arch. There are a number of other early churches with a combined corbel and semi-circular stone roof structure around the countryside including, St Doulagh's in north County Dublin and St Flannan's Oratory in Killaloe County Clare.

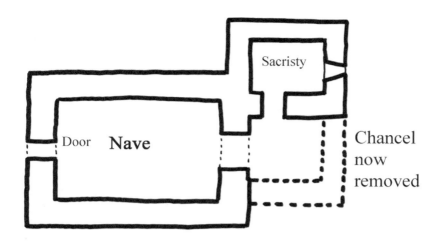

Fig.71: Plan, St Kevin's Church, Glendalough, County Wicklow.

Fig.72: St Kevin's church, Glendalough, County Wicklow.

ANTAE

In addition to the boat-shaped roof structures, there was another tradition in church design that seems to have been based on wooden forms, such as that on St MacDara's Island off the Galway coast, which has recently been restored. In this case, the little church consists of a single rectangular chamber about 5 metres by 4 metres. The outstanding feature here is that the side walls of the structure have been extended beyond the outer face of the gable walls to create a pillar-like projection, called 'antae' (Fig.73). These antae carry up both edges of the stone roof until they meet at the apex. A carved 'V'-shaped stone, or finial, sits at the apex and suggests that the lines of the antae cross one another. The purpose of the antae is uncertain, but it is a common feature of the Irish Early Christian churches, and may represent the stylistic survival of the wooden fame technology used in the construction of wooden churches. On the other hand, the inclusion of antae may simply be a decorative practice of the period. In addition to St MacDara's church, other sites where the use of antae can be seen include: Dalkey Island, off south County Dublin; Glendalough in County Wicklow, Tempull MacDuagh on the Aran Islands, Lorrah church in County Tipperary (Fig.74), and St Mel's church in Ardagh, County Longford. In the case of the latter, only the base of the walls of the structure survives, but the antae can clearly be seen.

Fig.73: St MacDara's church, County Galway.

Fig.74: Lorrah church,
County Tipperary.

ACCOMMODATION

Over time, and in a number of cases, the single-chamber church proved too small for the community's needs and the floor area had to be increased. This was achieved, first by adding a chancel, or separate altar space, to the end of an existing building; while in other cases, churches with integrated naves and chancels were built. Two examples will illustrate this: Teampull MacDuagh and Reefert church. Teampull MacDuach on Inishmore was built with a rectangular nave and antae. Later the area of the building was increased by adding a chancel to the east end and fitting it the space between the antae (Fig.75). In the case of Reefert church in Glendalough in County Wicklow, only the walls survive but the integrated form of the nave and chancel, which are separated by a semi-circular chancel arch, is clear (Fig.76).

At this point it is worth noting a number of the smaller elements that were commonly incorporated into the Early Christian churches. These include the wooden roofs, doors and windows. Where stone roofs were not used the churches were given wooden roofs. These consisted of 'A'-type wooden roof framing which was covered with the slates, wooden shingles or thatch. St Mary's, Temple na Skellig and Trinity churches in Glendalough, for example, all had wooden roofs. Trinity church even had a system of projecting stone brackets on the gable walls that carried and supported the ends of the wooden roof structure (Fig.77).

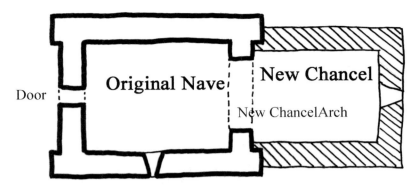

Fig. 75: Layout, nave with added chancel, Teampull MacDuagh, Inishmore, County Galway.

Original Nave

New Chancel

Door

New ChancelArch

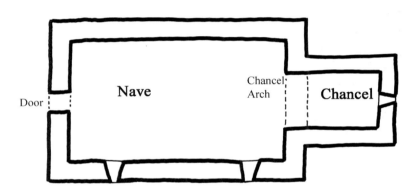

Fig. 76: Layout, integrated nave and chancel church, Reefert church, Glendalough, County Wicklow.

Nave

Chancel Arch

Chancel

Door

Fig.77: Corbelled roof bracket, Reefert church, Glendalough, County Wicklow.

DOOR AND WINDOW OPENINGS

Most of the church door openings were around a metre wide with slightly inward sloping sides and a stone lintel, or head. In a few cases the builders seem to have had some worry about the strength of the lintel and placed a stone relieving arch directly over the slab. The doorway to Reefert church in Glendalough, for instance, has a simple lintel over the opening (Fig.78), while the doorway in the nearby cathedral has a combination of lintel and overhead arch (Fig.79). The interior of most of the Early Christian churches must have been dark, to judge by the size of the window openings, most of which were little more than narrow slits, with flat or curved heads. Trinity church for example has two types of window heads. The simplest of these consists of two flat stones propped against one another to form a triangular headed opening (Fig.80). In the same building, a semi-circular opening was created by cutting the curved shape out of a single rectangular stone (Fig.81). Elsewhere in the same monastic complex, Reefert church has a small properly constructed arch made up of five wedge-shaped arch stones (Fig.82).

Fig.78: Doorway, Refert church, Glendalough, County Wicklow.

Fig.79: Doorway, cathedral,
Glandalough, County Wicklow.

Fig.80: Triangular headed window, Trinity church,
Glendalough, County Wicklow.

Fig.81: Round headed window, Trinity church, Glendalough, County Wicklow.

Fig.82: Window arch, Reefert church, Glendalough, County Wicklow.

ROUND TOWERS

There is one further building type that, more than any other, can be seen to represent Irish Early Christian architecture: the round tower. This consists essentially of a tall, slim, circular tower with a pointed roof, such as that in Glendalough (Fig.83) and Cashel in County Tipperary (Fig.84). Most examples are five, or more, storeys high, with a narrow slit window on each level and four larger windows on the top storey. The doorways are usually around 3 metres above ground level and inside a series of wooden floors joined by wooden ladders or stairs were provided. The wooden floors were constructed from boarding supported by wooden beams. Today, of course, these wooden structures have long since rotted, but the floors in Devinish in County Fermanagh, as well as those in Kilkenny and Kildare have been reconstructed and the visitor can climb to the top storey.

The purpose of the round towers has generated much speculation in the past, although it is now agreed that they were primarily bell towers, from which bells could be wrung at various time during the day. The likelihood is that the towers also acted as places of safety for storing the monastery valuables. This would account for the placing of the door a secure distance above the ground level. In such cases the tower could only be reached by means of a ladder or stairs. In terms of dimensions, most towers measure around 5 metres internally and rise to a height of around 30 metres. Close on 100 round towers survive around the country today, many with their pointed roofs intact. Amongst those are Ardmore, Cashel, Castledermot, Kells, Kilmacduagh, and Monasterboice, while examples

Fig.83: Round tower, Glendalough, County Wicklow.

Fig.84: Round tower, Cashel, County Tipperary.

like Clonmacnoise, Iniscealtra and Roscrea no longer have their top. The construction date of the towers remains uncertain, but the probability is that most were built between the ninth and twelve century.

In architectural terms, the monks and craftsmen of the Early Christian period can be viewed as attempting to develop an individual style of architecture: one that lay outside of Roman influence. This same historical and artistic period also saw considerable advances in the carving and decoration of masonry work, where considerable skill made its appearance in the creation of ogham stones, inscribed slabs and high crosses.

SEVEN

INSCRIPTIONS AND HIGH CROSSES

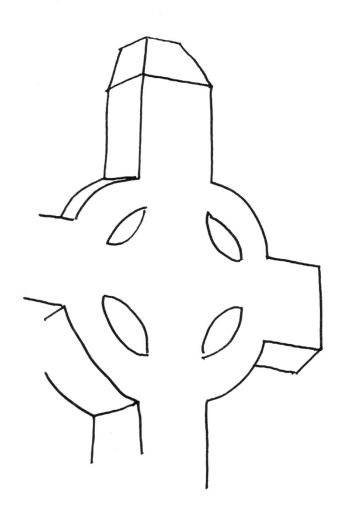

OGHAM STONES

The earliest stone carvings to express a definite Christian emphasis seem to have been Ogham stones. These were slender upright stones with a message carved along one of the sharp edges. The use of these type of stones probably date from around the fifth century or before and although the origins of this type of monument are unknown, they seem to have continued in use until about the eight century. They are commonly found in Irish sites with monastic connection, but not in any great numbers elsewhere. A number of isolated examples have been found in Scotland, the Isle of Man and Wales, and the probability is that these were the result of Early Irish Christian missionary activity.

The Ogham stone is of particular interest as it offers the first suggestion of both writing and Christianity in Ireland. It may well be that the origins of Ogham carving dates from the pre-Christian period – although this is uncertain. The typical example can vary in height from a little over a metre to over 3 metres tall, inscribed with a short message,

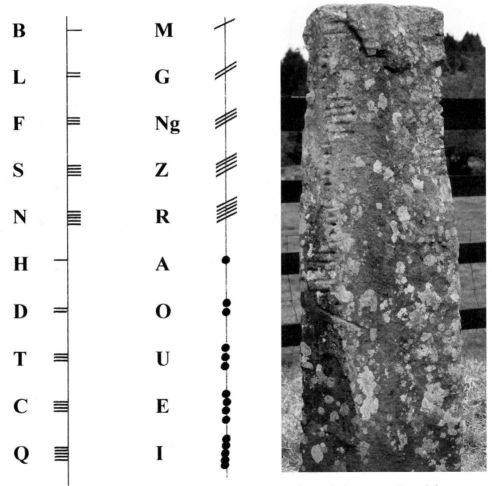

Fig.85: Ogham alphabet.

Fig.86: Ogham stone, Drumlohan, County Waterford.

usually in an early form of Gaelic. This message was mainly cut along the edge of the stone starting at the bottom and working upwards. The message preserved on one of the stones in the National Library in Dublin, for example, translates as, 'Fiachra son of Glunlegge'. The Ogham script itself can be considered as a type of code that was based on knowledge of the Latin alphabet. Instead of using the Latin script, each letter was represented by a series of short slashes cut into one edge of the stone (Fig.85).

Most of the Ogham stones discovered to date have been found primarily in the southern counties. Two hundred and eighty-five have been identified between counties Cork, Kerry and Waterford, while elsewhere there are twelve in County Kilkenny, eight each in counties Kildare and Mayo, and so far only one in County Wicklow. One of the clearest examples of Ogham script is on the range of stones that can be found in Drumlohan in County Waterford (Fig.86). These came from an adjacent souterrain, where they had been used as roof stones. They were recently removed from the souterrain and were erected in a standing position nearby (Fig.87). Today, the Ogham stones are arranged around the souterrain while other Ogham stones, which were used as uprights in the souterrain walling, remain in place (Fig.17).

Fig.87: Ogham stones and souterrain, Drumlohan, County Waterford.

CROSS-INSCRIBED SLABS

Perhaps the earliest type of monument with a definite link to Christianity are the cross-inscribed slabs, of which many variations exist all across the country. Essentially these consist of flat slabs of stone with a cross, or other religious symbol, inscribed on the surface. The monastic site at Glendalough, for instance, has a prominent example built into the wall near the entrance gate to the site. This is a large irregular boulder with a simple curved cross cut into the smooth face of the stone (Fig 88). The Glendalough site also has a wide range of inscribed slabs. Some of these are displayed in the visitor centre, while others can be found in various places around the site. In Clonmacnoise in County Offaly there is an extensive range of slabs on display. These range from a slim-looking cross with plain semi-circular ends and text on both sides (Fig.89), to a similar but more delicate example with complex curved decorated patterns at the centre and the ends of the stems (Fig.90).

Fig.88: Inscribed slab, Glendalough, County Wicklow.

Fig.89: Inscribed slab, Clonmacnoise, County Offaly.

Fig.90: Inscribed slab, Clonmacnoise, County Offaly.

HIGH CROSSES

It is, however, in the case of the high crosses that the highest level of Celtic stone carving was reached. These, as the name suggests, were tall slim stone crosses, often standing 4 or 5 metre high, which are sometimes referred to as Celtic Crosses. Apart from their height, the outstanding features of these crosses include the pronounced circular band at the intersection of the upright and arms of the cross; as well as an extraordinary level of masonry skill, in terms of human representation, and graphic images. The faces of the crosses were mainly decorated with Biblical scenes. The work on the east face usually focuses on scenes from the Old Testament, while that on the opposite face concentrates on the New Testament, with the Crucifixion filling the crossing. The sides also contained Biblical references as well as intricate patterns of interlaced ribbon work.

In terms of form, the high cross was made up of three parts: the plinth, the body, or shaft, and the cap stone (Fig.91). The base is usually around half a metre high. It is rectangular in plan but with the sides sloping inwards as it rises, like a wedge. Above this the main upright of the cross rises with a pronounced circular band, or ring, which

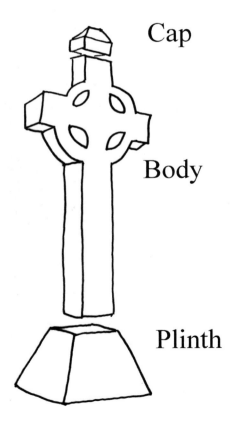

Cap

Body

Plinth

Fig.91: High cross elements.

accentuates the junction of the upright and the arms of the cross. The band itself is accentuated by the four small open spaces between the edges and the arms, all of which gave the high cross its characteristic 'Celtic' outline. Finally, the upright was topped with a small cap stone. This usually consists of a stylistic image of a house or church, complete with rectangular sides, high pitched gables, and slated roof, such as the fine example on Muiredach's Cross in Monasterboice, County Louth (Fig.92). The purpose of carving and erecting the high cross seems to have been complex. The Biblical focus express a clear religious purpose, perhaps as a memorial to a founder, or an illustrated Biblical teaching devise. In other cases the crosses may have acted as boundary markers. In any event, there is little doubt that they expressed the success and wealth of individual monasteries. Little is known about the historic development of the crosses. The idea may have been based on earlier wooden examples, or developed from the inscribed slabs by the gradual increase in scale. Alternatively, the idea of the monumental stone cross may have been imported from mainland Europe and went on to develop distinctive Irish characteristics. Whatever the case, there is little evidence to act as a guide, except that the bulk of the examples seem to date from around the ninth century, with a later

Fig.92: Cap stone, Muiredach's Cross, Monasterboice, County Louth.

group emerging around the twelfth century. This ninth century date is suggested by the inscription on the cross at Kinnity in County Offaly, which has an inscription at the base stating it was erected by King Maelsechnaill between 846 and 862. It is also probable that there were localised schools of cross production, but whether these reflect different time scales is uncertain.

Many of the high crosses can be found in clusters, marking the site of Early Christian communities, although occasionally single crosses are all that survive. Amongst the clusters, those at Castledermot, Kells, Glendalough, Clonmacnoise, Durrow, Kilfenora, Monasterboice, and Moone offer outstanding examples. Elsewhere, isolated crosses can be found in Ardboe, Clones, Finglas, and Termonfeckin. In visual terms, the high cross can be classified into four types: early crosses, vertically-emphasised crosses, ring-emphasised crosses, and figure-based crosses. It must, however, be stressed that this classification is based on visual grounds, and has no historical developmental significance. Rather it offers a comparative way of viewing the various examples.

EARLY CROSSES

The tall inscribed cross at Cardonagh in County Donegal seems to offer an intermediate stage between an inscribed slab and a high cross (Fig.93). The front panels probably represent

Fig.93: Inscribed high cross, Carndonagh, County Donegal.

Fig 94: Early cross, Rathmichael, County Dublin.

the Crucifixion. Christ is the largest figure, with the two thieves, on either side. The lower figures probably represent the Apostles or the Holy Women. Above this, a wide ribbon-like interlaced pattern fills the space where the stubby arms and the upright of the cross intersect. On the far side, the cross is filled with another wide ribbon-like interlaced pattern. A more developed, but smaller, cross is located near the Early Christian site at Rathmichael in County Dublin. Here the low cross has a large solid central ring that carries the figure of the crucified Christ on both sides, but with the cross arms barely represented (Fig. 94).

VERTICALLY-EMPHASISED CROSSES

In the case of the vertically-emphasised crosses, height is the main feature. For example, good examples of this vertical emphasis can be noted at Castledermot, Moon and Monasterboice. Castledermot in County Kildare has two splendid crosses cut from granite, although in both cases the cap stone is missing. Each cross is decorated with a series of Biblical and decorative

Fig.95: High cross, Moone, County Kildare.

panels. Those on the North Cross include Adam and Eve, King David, and Daniel in the Lions Den. Both the back and the base of the cross are decorated with spiral designs. The South Cross is similarly arranged in panels that include the crucifixion and the arrest of Christ, while lower down the base depicts the Loaves and Fishes. Here the back of the cross is decorated with a range of spiral, interlaced and geometric panels. Also in County Kildare, the cross in Moon has recently been restored and displays a wonderful range of Old and New Testament panel (Fig.95). The shaft is particularly high and is decorated with a range of fresh looking scenes including the Flight into Egypt, the Loaves and Fishes, and the twelve apostles (Fig.96). The West Cross in Monasterboice, is one of the tallest of the high crosses, standing over 7 metres high (Fig.97). It has a series of panels on the west side recounting the life and crucifixion of Christ, with a range of Biblical scenes on the far side. The base in undecorated and the cap stone is in place.

Fig.96: Base, high cross, Moone, County Kildare.

Fig.97: High Cross, Clonmacnoise, County Ofally.

RING-EMPHASISED CROSSES

The distinguishing feature of the ring-emphasised crosses is that the intersects cross the upright about half way up the shaft and the crossing is emphasised by being surrounded by a large circle. This gives the crosses like those in Ahenny and Kilkieran a stubby appearance. The South Cross at Ahenny in County Tipperary is one of a pair of similar design (Fig.98). The faces of both crosses are covered with intricate interlacing designs with five pronounced circular stud-like projections. The South Cross is almost 4 metres high, while the nearby North Cross is a little shorter at just over 3 metres high. Both crosses have dome-like cap stones and the only figure carving is on the bases, which in both instances is difficult to interpret. The three crosses at Kilkieran in County Kilkenny are similar in scale and form to those at Ahenny. Here, the crosses carry the same form of interlaced panels, circular studs and figure sculpture on the base. These crosses also feature conical cap stones.

Fig.98: High cross, Ahenny, County Tipperary.

FIGURE-BASED CROSSES

During the twelfth century there seems to have been a change in the approach to the form of the carving, although what prompted the change in not known. Essentially the Biblical scenes with their accompanying decorations were replaced with single realistic figures of Christ. The cross at Dysert O'Dea in County Clare for example has three parts (Fig.99). The base is rectangular with inward sloping sides and interlaced ribbons. Above this, the shaft contains a lifelike, but undecorated religious figure, possible a bishop, complete with a mitre and crosier. Above this the main face of the cross bears the figure of the crucified Christ with outstretched arms. There is a line of decorative beading around the edge of the cross. The back of the cross is decorated with a range of geometric panels as well as interlaced animals and human figures. The high cross in Tuam in County Galway is currently positioned in the centre of the town. It is more complex than the Dysert O'Dea example. The base contains an ecclesiastical figure on both sides, while above this the

Fig.99: High cross, Dysert O'Dea, County Clare.

upright is decorated with interlaced panels. Further up, one face carries the figure of Christ with an ecclesiastical figure on the opposite side.

BULLAUN STONES

There was one other interesting, if puzzling, form of carved stone that emerged in the Early Christian period. This was the bullaun stone and it is nearly always associated with Early Christian sites. This type of monument consists of a large irregular boulder with cup-shaped hollow carefully cut into it. The shape is always circular, measures around 150 millimetres across and about half that in depth. The fact that most of these stones can be found in, or near, religious sites suggests the stone had a religious function, although a number of examples can be found in total isolation. These may be the sole remnant of a monastic sites, where all other evidence of religious occupation has disappeared.

The typical bullaun stone carries a single cup shape, although stones with several closely spaced cups are not unusual. One of the bullaun stones in Glendalough has a single basin (Fig. 100), while that at Aghowle in the same county has four cups closely spaced together (Fig. 101). This variation presents difficulties in deciding what purpose the bullaun stone served. Certainly, the care and precision with which the cup shapes were cut into the stone

Fig. 100: Single-basin bullaun stone, Glendalough, County Wicklow.

Fig. 101: Four-basin bullaun stone, Aghowle, County Wicklow.

suggests an important function. The use of the cups for grinding or for holding holy water has been suggested, although the question as to why some boulders have a single cup, while others have a number remains unanswered.

One of the curious differences between the Early Christian churches and the high crosses of the same period is that of decoration. Whereas the high crosses and the inscribed slabs – and indeed the decorated manuscripts and metalwork of the period – carry a high level of applied decoration, most of the early church buildings lack any form of decoration. Why this was the case is uncertain. The twelfth century, however, saw a dramatic change in this approach to church decoration, with the arrival and adoption of the Romanesque style in Ireland.

EIGHT

THE ROMANESQUE

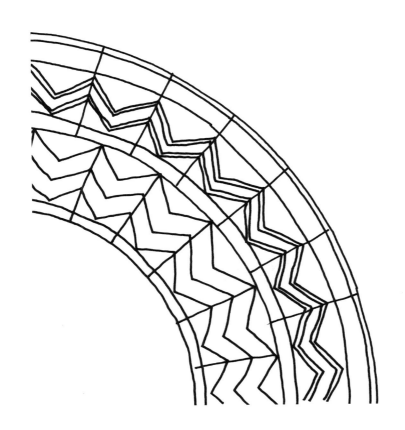

ROMANESQUE

The Romanesque movement seems to have first appeared in Ireland when work began on Cormac's Chapel, on the Rock of Cashel in County Tipperary in around 1127. This was a style of architecture that had developed in Continental Europe and England and had three main ingredients. These included layout, structure and decoration. In order to appreciate the significance of this style for Irish Early Christian architecture, it is necessary to understand these ingredients.

In terms of layout, the Continental and English Romanesque churches were built to a standard basilica plan. This consisted of a nave, side isles, and a chancel. The nave was the main body of the church and was rectangular in plan. This was usually flanked on each side by a side aisle, which was connected to the nave by a system of arched openings or arcades. The chancel was the rectangular or semi-circular altar space which was located on the east end of the nave and separated from it by a wide chancel arch. Another common feature of Continental church layout was the inclusion of tall bell towers – often flanking one another on either side of the church.

Fig.102: Romanesque chancel arch, Nun's church, Clonmacnoise, County Offaly.

The main structural element of the Romanesque church was the use of the stone semi-circular arch. This was extensively used throughout the building, for example in the arcades between the aisles and the nave, the ceilings, the chancel arch, the doorways and the windows. In addition to the semi-circular arch itself, it was the decoration applied to the faces of the arches that characterised the Romanesque. Essentially the Romanesque arch consisted of several arches, or orders, placed one inside the other – all of which were elaborately decorated with deeply cut zigzag, or cheurgin. In Irish terms, the chancel arch of the ruined Nun's church in Clonmacnoise offers an outstanding example of the Romanesque arch. Here the arch has three orders, with elaborate zigzag patterns (Fig. 102).

CORMAC'S CHAPEL

In the case of Cormac's Chapel, only some of the standard Romanesque features were used and even then in a restrained fashion. The plan consisted of a nave, chancel and a pair of towers on each side of the nave (Fig. 103). The church was tiny indeed when compared to the contemporary English and Continental Romanesque examples. The towers are small and projected outwards at the point where the nave met the chancel. This gives the plan a cruciform shape. The tower on the south side contains a circular stairs to the overhead croft, while the other seems to have acted as a sacristy. Despite its small size, the church had two doorways, one on each side of the nave, although the south doorway was probably a later insertion. Internally, the church is richly decorated by an elaborate system of wall arcades,

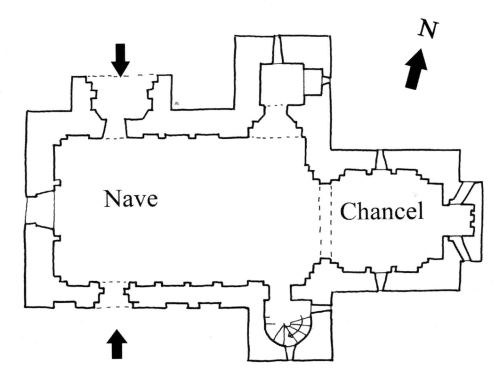

Fig. 103: Layout, Cornmac's Chapel, Cashel, County Tipperary.

made up mainly of Romanesque arches and columns, set into the blank side walling. The lines of the columns are projected upwards and cross under the semi-circular ceiling, in the form of ribs. These divide the ceiling into a series of bays (Fig. 104). The interior was originally lit by three round-headed windows in the west wall, but these were later built up, when the adjoining cathedral was erected in the thirteenth century.

Externally the church is very dramatic looking indeed, particularly within the modest context of the Irish Romanesque movement. The external walling is divided into a sequence of storeys by projecting bands, or string courses, and positioned between the string courses are a range of arched blank arcading. The south doorway sits unevenly into the arcade pattern and consists of three orders of columns and arches, while the opposite north doorway is highly decorated with six orders of columns and arches. Above this

Fig. 104: Interior, Cornmac's Chapel, Cashel, County Tipperary.

is a large triangular gable, or pediment, is also decorated by lines of zigzag carving and rose-like emblems. The construction of the roof followed the early Irish practice and consisted of a steeply pitched stone corbelled structure, underneath which is a small croft. The floor of the croft acts as both a supporting arch for the corbelled roof structure and the semi–circular ceiling to the nave. To complete the composition the heights of the towers are emphasised by a series of string courses which have blank arcading at the fourth level (Fig. 105).

The building of Cormac's Chapel seems to have had a significant impact on the Irish monastic communities of the period and prompted the spread of the Romanesque style around the country. This emerged in two forms. First where established churches were remodelled and secondly where completely new churches

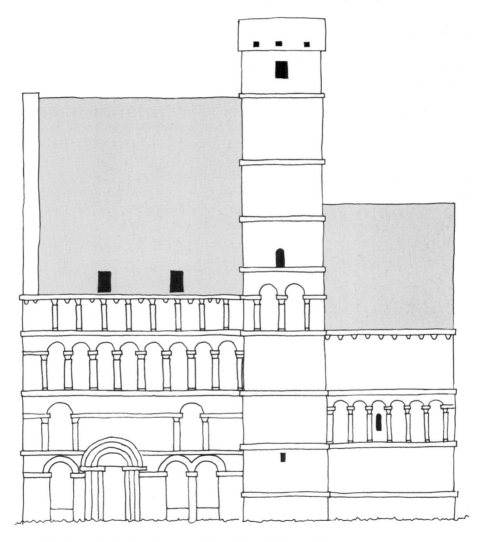

Fig. 105: Sketch, south elevation, Cormac's Chapel, Cashel, County Tipperary.

were built. These Irish Romanesque churches, however, differed in two ways from their European and English counterparts. Firstly, they are infinitely smaller and secondly the Irish builders seem never to have applied the Romanesque in a unified manner. Instead, the Romanesque techniques were used only as a form of decoration. In most Irish examples, the typical Romanesque style semi-circular arch was used, but the basilica plan with its elaborate use of arches, ribs and vaults, so characteristic of the British and Continental Romanesque never found favour. The Irish Romanesque, therefore, is characterised by the use of modest simple structures with stone and wooden roofs, as well as round-headed doors, windows and chancel arches, with Romanesque style decoration. Notwithstanding this, a number of delightful Irish Romanesque churches were completed, amongst which notable examples can be found in Ardfert and Kilmalkedar in County Kerry, Killaloe and Iniscealtra in County Clare, Clonmacnoise and Rahan in County Offaly, and Glendalough in County Wicklow, although regrettably, most examples of the Irish Romanesque survive today only as ruins.

IRISH ROMANESQUE CHURCHES

Judging by its simplicity, St Caimin's church in Iniscealtra is one of the earliest of the Irish churches to embrace the Romanesque. This church began as a single-chamber building with antae, measuring around 30 metres long and 6 metres wide, and possibly dating from around AD 1000. During the twelfth century, a number of alterations were carried out to the structure. A chancel and chancel arch were added to the east side of the building, in addition to which a new doorway was inserted into the west gable – all in an early Romanesque style (Fig.106). The chancel arch consists of three undecorated plain orders, with a single head-shaped keystone on the outermost arch (Fig.107). This lack of decoration, suggest an early date for the completion of the work. The columns underneath the arches are equally unadorned except for the light carving on the column tops, or the capitals, and the bases.

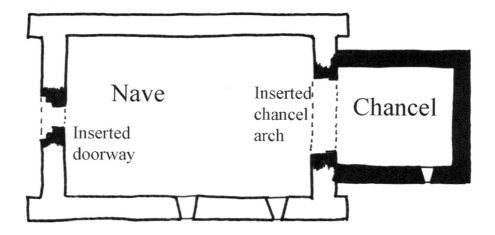

Fig.106: Plan, St Caimin's church, Iniscealtra, County Clare.

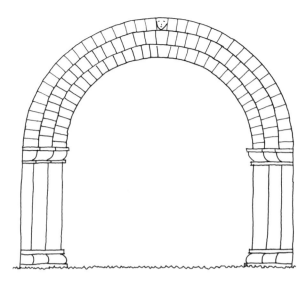

Fig. 107: Chancel arch, St Caimin's church, Iniscealtra, County Clare.

Fig. 108: Nun's church, Clonmacnoise, County Offaly.

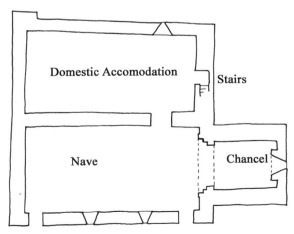

Fig. 109: Layout, St Saviour's Priory, Glendalough, County Wicklow.

In contrast, the Nun's church in Clonmacnoise, offer one of the more developed examples of the Irish Romanesque. Here the church has the well preserved remains of a doorway and the chancel arch, but little else of the structure survives (Fig. 108). The doorway has four orders with accentuated animal-headed capitals. The arches have particularly deep chevron patterns, motifs that are repeated on one of the supporting columns, while the chancel arch is made up of three orders with dramatic chevron patterns, curved columns, as well as complex geometric capitals and floral-like bases (Fig. 102).

The ruined St Saviour's Priory in Glendalough, lies a little down the valley from the main monastic site and is said to have been founded in 1162. The walling of the nave and chancel partially survives as do the walls of the small adjoining domestic building (Fig. 109). The building has been much altered, but the chancel arch (Fig. 110) and the east window (Fig. 111) offers an excellent range of Romanesque carvings including human and animal faces as well as the characteristic chevron, roll and geometric patterns. The jambs of the chancel arch are decorated with semi-circular mouldings and geometric panels, while the bottom triangular panel on each side has stylistic animal and human form (Fig. 112). Unfortunately some of this work has weathered considerably.

The unroofed church at Kilmalkedar in County Kerry is one of the few Irish examples that incorporate internal arcading. The nave is around 7 metres long with antae on the gable walls (Fig. 113). The west door has three orders of elaborately decorated columns and chevron arches, while the chancel arch is equally elaborately decorated with two orders.

Fig. 110: Chancel arch, St Saviour's Priory, Glendalough, County Wicklow.

Fig.111: East window, St Saviour's Priory, Glendalough, County Wicklow.

Fig.112: Chancel arch jamb, St Saviour's Priory, Glendalough, County Wicklow.

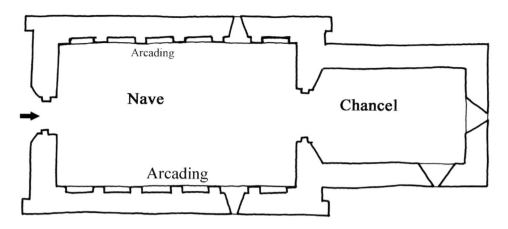

Fig.113: Plan, Kilmalkedar church, County Kerry.

Fig.114: Internal arcading, Kilmalkedar church, County Kerry.

An unusual feature is the arcading that runs along the inside of the nave walls. This consists of half rounded columns with blank panels between, all built into the walling. The rhythm set up by the arcading is, however, disrupted by the arrangement of the single window on each side of the nave. These are higher than the arcade panels and have splayed jambs and arched heads (Fig. 114).

SURVIVING ELEMENTS

In a number of Irish Romanesque churches, little survives except for ruined and isolated elements. For example, the external arcading and gables, but little else, survives of the Romanesque churches in Roscrea, County Tipperary and Ardmore in County Waterford. In the case of the St Cronan's in Roscrea, the impressive west front of the church consists of a wide gable, with a five-bay arched arcade set between the antae (Fig. 115).

Fig. 115: West facade, St Cronan's church, Roscrea, County Tipperary.

The central bay acts as a focus to the entrance door and it is made up of three orders of columns and arches, with deep chevron decorations on the arches. Above the arch, a tall triangular pediment contains the figure of a bishop, or an abbot. On either side of this central bay, the remainder of the arcade is made of a similar arrangement of blank arches and pediments, only smaller in scale than the entrance.

In terms of uniqueness, the external arcade on the west gable of the ruined Ardmore Cathedral is the most outstanding. This consists of a double line of arcades, arranged one above the other (Fig. 116). The upper arcade consists of thirteen blank arches, or niches, some containing carvings of Biblical scenes. In contrast, the lower arcade is composed of two large semi-circular arches, with a system of round-headed niches set into each one. Some of the niches contain Biblical scenes. Unfortunately, weathering has blurred much of the stone surface and this has made the interpretation of many of the panels difficult.

In the case of both Killeshin church and Clonfert Cathedral, a particularly high level of Romanesque craftsmanship went into the creation of the west doorways. The doorway of Killeshin in County Laois is one of the most elaborate of the Irish Romanesque period (Fig. 117). The arched doorway and jambs are each divided into four orders. These have rounded columns with bulb-like decorated bases and elaborate

Fig. 116: West facade, cathedral, Ardmore, County Waterford.

Fig. 117: (Left) West doorway, Killeshin, County Laois.

Fig. 118: (Right) West doorway, Clonfert Cathedral, County Galway.

97

capitals. The four semi-circular arches are made up of a range of dramatic chevron and geometric patterns. The doorway was given a triangular pediment, but this was in recent times.

The doorway to the much altered Clonfert Cathedral in County Galway is, without question, the most outstanding example of the Irish Romanesque movement. It is composed of an outer elaborately carved architrave with five orders of columns inside this. Each of these is again elaborately decorated with geometric and zigzag patterns. Above the columns, a corresponding number of arches are decorated in an astonishing range of elements including, chevrons, floral and geometric motives (Fig. 118). Above the arches is a triangular pediment which is equally astonishing. The bottom section of the pediment has a row of arches and columns, with human heads filing the arches. Above this the remainder of the pediment is divided into small triangles. These are made up of alternating geometric designs and human heads. All in all, the level of achievement in Killeshin and Clonfert must be regarded as the high point Irish Romanesque masonry work.

NINE

CELTIC MONASTERIES

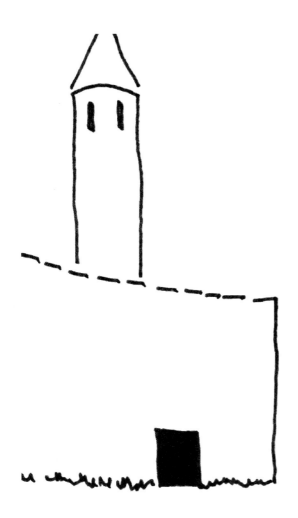

MONASTERIES

Having looked at the development of church architecture and stone sculpture in the Early Christian and Romanesque periods, it is appropriate to close the guide with an overview of these elements and how they were combined to produce the characteristic Early Christian monastery. In terms of location, most of the monastic sites were established in less populated areas of the countryside and consisted of circular or oval enclosures, inside which the community service buildings were erected. The layout of these enclosures seems to have been based on the ring, or stone forts of the period, with their protective walls and trenches. The probability is that, particularly in the earlier cases, the monks or nuns made use of established ring-forts: perhaps donated to the community by a local chieftain. In later cases the communities may have laid out and raised their enclosures on green field sites. The time scale during which these communities were established probably extended between AD 500 and AD 1150, although this is not certain.

FORM

The reason for the choice of the ring-fort form for the enclosure is uncertain, but it probably marked the physical boundary between the religious community and the outside world. Also, of course, it provided protection from wild animals or raiders. Inside the shelter of the walls, the huts, churches, and workshops of the community were laid out. The placing of the buildings and their relationship with one another within the enclosure seems not to have followed any rigid plan. Nevertheless two features seemed to have remained constant. These are the circular or oval plan and an eastern approach route. The reasoning behind of the eastern approach is not known, nor was its use universal. Most of the monastic sites have this eastern orientation, but a number, such as Finglas in County Dublin, seem to have had their approach on the western side. The diagrammatic sketch in Figure 119 offers a simple illustration of what an early monastery may have looked like. The illustration includes a small number of buildings for clarity, but in reality a monastery such as this may have had many more huts and buildings, both inside and outside the enclosure.

SCALE

In the case of the more successful monasteries, the area of the initial enclosure soon proved too small for the expanding community and the site area had to be enlarged. This was achieved in a number of ways. A second larger enclosure was laid out beyond the line of the original space, establishing an inner and outer enclosure, one outside the other. The monastery at Kells in County Meath for example was laid out in this fashion. In cases like this, the inner enclosure seems to have acted as the religious core of the monastery. It contained a range of religious buildings including churches, cells, high-crosses, a cemetery, and in the more prosperous examples, a round tower. The outer enclosure on the other hand seems to have fulfilled a more secular function and seems to have possessed craft and workshop facilities as well as religious buildings. Elsewhere, larger monasteries like Nendrum in County Down, progressed to such a stage that they required three enclosures, one outside the other. In the case of Killeigh in County Offaly a second enclosure was attached to the side of the original complex, creating a figure-of-eight arrangement. In other instances communities decided to

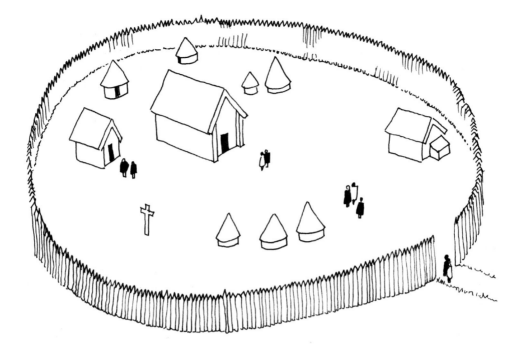

Fig. 119: Diagrammatic sketch, typical Early Christian monastery.

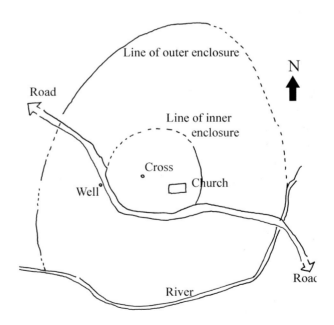

Fig. 120: Plan, Early Christian
Monastery, Lorrha, County
Tipperary.

establish a second enclosure, adjacent to but separate from the initial site. Examples of this form of arrangement include the monasteries at Clonmacnoise, Glendalough and Kilkenny, where some distance separates the two enclosures.

When looking at the Early Christian sites today, it is necessary to remember that, just like the ring-forts, the sites offer only a shadow of their initial form. The wooden churches and other buildings have all perished without trace. In addition, the stockades have rotted away and the banks have very often collapsed into the trenches. Remarkably, the circular lines of the enclosures very often survive into the present, although in a reduced scale. Even in cases where the stone buildings survive they are mostly in ruins. Significantly, the great majority of these early monastic sites have remained in active service as cemeteries well into recent times and today the number of such sites that remain on the landscape stretches into four figures. Most of these were small in scale and include, for example, those at Aghowle and Lorrha (Fig. 120) as well as Kilvoydan (Fig. 121) in County Clare where the form of the oval enclosure and eastern approach route still survive.

In Aghowle in County Wicklow, the line of the inner enclosure follows an uneven oval course, although the outer enclosure, if it ever existed, has disappeared. Inside the enclosure, the walls of an early Romanesque church and an uncompleted high cross stand surrounded by ancient and modern gravestones. The bullaun stone (Fig. 101) that lies well outside the enclosure line offers a hint that the site may have had an outer enclosure at one time. In the case of Lorrha in County Tipperary the lines of the inner and outer enclosures partially survive. Here the monastery was founded by St Rodhan in the sixth century. In the case of the inner enclosure, the curved east boundary is defined by the line of an earthen bank, while the south and west line is defined by the curve of the roadway. Inside the enclosure the antiquity of the site is emphasised by the remains of a church with antae, as well as the remains of a high cross. The line of the outer enclosure can be identified on the west side by field boundaries and on the south by the course of a small river.

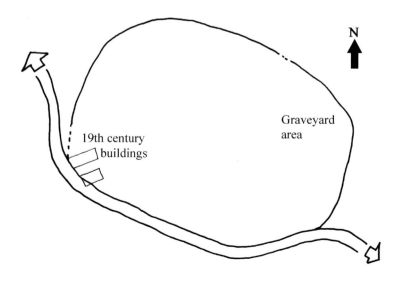

Fig. 121: Early Christian monastery, Kilvoydan, County Clare.

In a number of cases, the circular enclosure line has disappeared and only sections of the monastic architecture survive on the landscape. It may be that the original enclosure was built with wood and perished over time, to be replaced later with a rectangular boundary. In Old Kilcullen in County Kildare, for example, the site has a rectangular low stone-wall boundary. The reason for this is uncertain. However, the surviving fabric inside the walling testifies to the site's Early Christian origins. This includes the stump of a small church, the lower half of a round tower, the bases of two high crosses, as well as a range of contemporary grave stones. Alternatively, the site may have been given a rectangular shape originally. This choice might have been based on some geographical or prevailing restriction at the time. Skellig Michael off the County Kerry coast, for example, has a rectangular enclosure, which was dictated by the physical irregularity of the site.

STONE-BUILT MONASTERIES

In cases where monasteries were built with stone, much more of the original fabric survive and this offers a more understandable example of how a monastery looked. Amongst the more notable examples of these stone built monasteries are Innishmurray in County Sligo, Illauntannig and Skellig Michael in County Kerry, and Glendalough in County Wicklow.

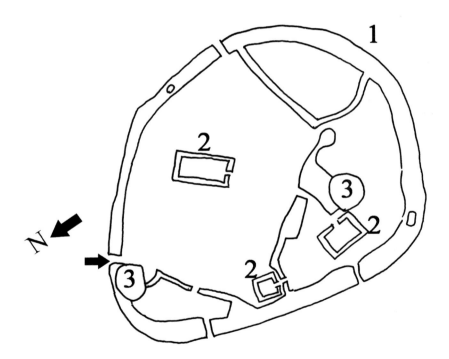

Fig. 122: Sketch layout, Early Christian monastery, Inishmurray, County Sligo.
1. Enclosure
2. Churches
3. Beehive Huts

One of the best preserved of the small stone-built monasteries is that on the island of Inishmurray, off the County Sligo coast (Fig. 122). The foundation here has been attributed to St Molaise during the sixth century. The monastery plan is oval in outline and the enclosing stone wall survives intact. The wall thickness varies between a metre and 2 metres wide and stands almost 4 metres high. The wall also incorporates a number of small wall chambers, as well as a souterrain. Access to the interior of the monastery is provided by a number of narrow low entrance passageways and within the enclosure, the monastery is divided into four sectors by low stone walls. The largest sector contains the remains of two small churches; one with a stone roof, the other is unroofed but has antae on the east side. eest of this, a smaller sector contains the ruins of another small church and a beehive hut clustered together. There is also a second beehive hut, tucked into one corner of the small third northern sector (Fig. 123). The interior also possesses three solid table-like structures which may have acted as altars. The origin of these structures is uncertain and it may be that they date from a much later period.

ILLAUNTANNIG

Illauntannig is a cliff-edge island site in County Kerry. Here the foundation has been attributed to St Senan, although today only half the enclosure wall remains. Despite this,

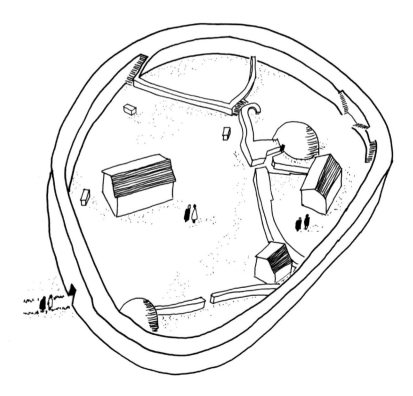

Fig. 123: Diagrammatic sketch, Early Christian monastery, Inishmurray, County Sligo.

it is still possible to make out the extent of the oval enclosure that measures around 30 metres, or thereabouts, at its widest part (Fig.124). The surviving sections of the masonry enclosure measures as much as 5 metres high at one point, but much of it is now collapsed. Inside the walls, the unroofed remains of a small rectangular church and three unroofed beehive huts survive. In addition, the enclosure walling contains two wall chambers and a narrow entrance passageway. There is also a souterrain running from one of the huts that extends beneath the enclosure wall. In addition, there are a number of small stone-built altar-like structures, much like Inishmurray, distributed around the enclosure.

SKELLIG MICHAEL

Skellig Michael is undoubtedly the most romantic and spectacular of the Early Christian sites. It is perched near the ridge of a massive jagged rock that rises up from the Atlantic Ocean, off the coast of County Kerry (Fig.125). Here a narrow irregular shelf of rock, about 200 metres above the sea was all that was available to the monks and they laid out two rectangular enclosures. These were located side by side but on different levels, with one above the other (Fig.126). Each of these was enclosed by an irregular stone wall. The

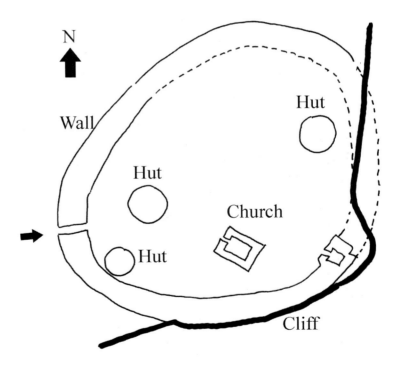

Fig.124: Sketch layout, Early Christian monastery, Illauntannig, County Kerry.

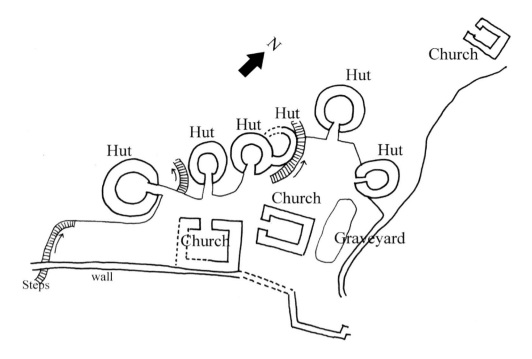

Fig.125: Sketch layout, Early Christian monastery, Skellig Michael, County Kerry.

Fig.126: Entrance, Early Christian monastery, Skellig Michael, County Kerry.

Fig. 127: Early Christian monastery, Skellig Michael, County Kerry.

lower enclosure is entered by a narrow roofed passage, while another tunnel-like entrance links both of the enclosures together. Inside the upper enclosure the monks laid out a tight cluster of three small rectangular churches and six beehive huts, only one of which has lost its corbelled roof (Fig. 127).

GLENDALOUGH

In contrast to the modest scale of most Early Christian sites, there were a number that developed extensively. These include Glendalough, Clonmacnoise, Armagh, Kells, and Kildare. Of these, Glendalough in County Wicklow is one of the largest and displays a remarkable range of Early Christian and Romanesque churches, high crosses, inscribed slabs and a round tower. The name Glendalough translates as the 'glen of the two lakes' and it is here that St Kevin is credited with establishing the monastery in the sixth century. The approach road is from the east and it follows a line along the north side of the lakes, with the monastic remains distributed along the south side of the road. Today the Glendalough complex is made up of two independent sectors, separated from one another by the Lower

Lake (Fig. 128). Unfortunately, as is generally the case, all of the Glendalough buildings, with the exception of the round tower, are in ruins.

The upper sector has been credited as being the initial site of the monastery, but there is little evidence to support this. There is no evidence of an enclosure and today the sector includes a range of individual elements loosely scattered around an area on the south side the Upper Lake. These include the ruins of Temple-na-Skellig and Reefert churches, the base of a third church, the base of a small ring-fort, the stump of a beehive hut, a high cross, and a range of inscribed slabs and crosses. Temple-na-Skellig is the most westerly of the churches and consists of a small rectangular single chamber structure. The building is perched on a small platform that overlooks the lake and is one of the two Glendalough sites that are difficult to access. A little further along the lake edge there is a small man-made cave that sits high up on the rock face. This is called St Kevin's Bed and is often regarded as the cell in which St Kevin lived, although archaeological investigation suggests a much earlier date for its creation. Access here is also very difficult. Further east along the lake front, on a high point overlooking the water, there is the base of a small beehive hut, about which little is known (Fig. 129). This is also traditionally regarded as St Kevin's home, although there is no evidence to support this.

A little further east of the cell is Reefert church. This is a nave and chancel church with a semi-circular door, window and chancel arch (Figs. 77, 78, 82). The church is set on a roughly rectangular terrace, which contains a range of cross slabs and a high cross. The base of both the rectangular church (Fig. 130) and the ring-fort (Fig. 6) are positioned near the eastern edge of the lake, while distributed randomly around the same area are the stone crosses.

The lower sector of Glendalough, in contrast, follows a more conventional early-monastic double enclosure type of layout. Here the oval outer enclosure is defined by the curved course of two small rivers (Fig. 131), while the inner enclosure seems to have partially survived particularly along the course of the curved southern line. There is little evidence of a stone-built outer perimeter, although the impressive gate house still partly survives (Fig. 132). This seems to have been a double-storey structure with a semi circular archway through the building, although it is now unroofed. Within the inner enclosure are the cathedral, the round tower, and the Priests House.

The cathedral is the largest of the Glendalough structures. The original building consisted of a single nave with a plain flat-headed doorway and antae (Fig. 79). During some later period the structure was altered and extended. The height of the original walling was raised and a new chancel and sacristy was added to the east side. This work included the insertion of a wide Romanesque chancel arch, of which only the ends now survive.

The round tower remains intact and stands a little over 30 metres high. The plain arched doorway is around 3 metres over the round level. Above the doorway, the tower is provided with natural light by a system of slit windows in the shaft and four round headed windows at the top storey (Fig. 83). The Priests House is a small rectangular Romanesque building. The small scale of the structure suggests that this may have been a shrine rather than a church or oratory. There is a narrow doorway on the south side with carved triangular lintel overhead, although the stone is much damaged. The Romanesque feature is the semi-circular west window carrying zigzag decorations.

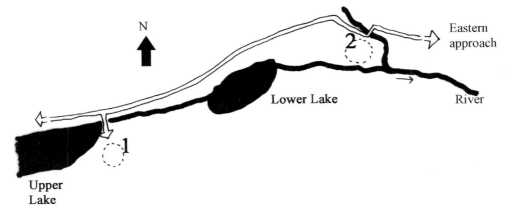

Fig. 128: Sketch layout, Early Christian monastery complex, Glendalough, County Wicklow.
1. Upper Lake sector
2. Lower Lake sector

Fig. 129: Beehive hut, Early Christian monastery, Glendalough, County Wicklow.

St Mary's, St Kevin's and St Kieran's churches were all laid out outside the inner enclosure, but inside the outer enclosure. St Mary's church is a plain single-chamber church with a flat-headed west doorway. Some time after its initial construction a chancel was added to the east side that almost doubled the floor area. Lightly decorated windows were inserted in the north and south walls, but the chancel arch no longer exists. St Kevin's church is one of the most individual of the Glendalough churches with its stone roof, round tower and surviving sacristy (Figs.71–72). South of St Kevin's church, all that remains of St Kieran's small nave and chancel church is the base of the walls and a small altar stone.

In addition to the buildings within the enclosures, two outer churches were built further down the valley. These are Trinity church and St Saviour's Priory. Trinity church lies a little to the east of the main enclosure and can be accessed from the approach road. The church originally had a nave and chancel plan to which an additional chamber was later added to the west end. The roof of this chamber incorporated a small round tower, much like that on the nearby St Kevin's church. Unfortunately, the tower was blown down in a storm in 1818 and little now survives. Elsewhere the structure has a range of small windows (Figs.80–81). The chancel arch and the west doorway have plain arched heads, while the door to the added chamber has a flat head. Much further down the valley the

Fig.130: Base of church, Early Christian monastery, Glendalough, County Wicklow.

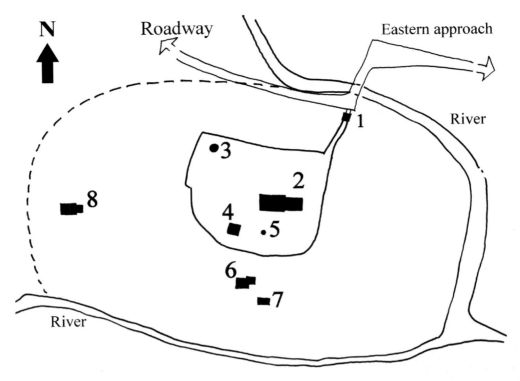

Fig.131: Sketch layout, lower sector, Early Christian monastery, Glendalough, County Wicklow.

1: Gatehouse
2: Cathedral
3: Round Tower
4: Priest's House
5: High Cross
6: St Kevin's church
7: St Keiran's church

most easterly of the Glendalough churches, St Saviour's Priory, can be found. This offers an excellent example of the Irish Romanesque and consists of a nave, chancel and an adjoining domestic chamber (Fig.109), with a range of highly decorated Romanesque arches and decorations (Figs.111-112).

In addition to the architecture, the Glendalough complex has an extensive range of crosses, inscribed slabs and bullaun stones. St Kevin's Cross stand unfinished on the south side of the cathedral. It caries no decoration and the openings of the rings seem not to have been completed. The inscribed slabs, a number of low crosses and a few bullaun stones are distributed randomly around the site. Elsewhere, the most significant of the slabs are displayed in the visitor centre and in St Kevin's church.

Fig.132: Gateway, Early Christian monastery, Glendalough, County Wicklow.

CLONMACNOISE

The layout of Clonmacnoise, in County Offaly, is more concentrated than Glendalough with the result that the buildings seem bundled closer together within a single enclosure. This is irregular in form with sharp rectangular sides, although whether this is the original enclosure line is uncertain. There is no evidence of any outer enclosures, although almost certainly at least one existed. There is also an outlying enclosure around 500 metres to the north east, which also has an irregular enclosure line. Within the main enclosure there is a range of churches, high crosses and a pair of round towers (Fig.133). The high crosses are

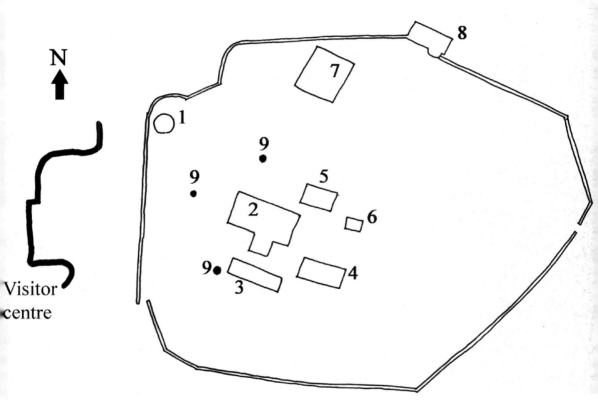

Fig.133: Sketch layout, Early Christian site, Clonmacnoise, County Offaly.
1: Round Tower
2: Cathedral
3: Temple Doolin
4: Temple Melaghlin
5: Temple Kelly
6: Temple Ciaran
7: Temple Connor
8: Temple Finghin and Round Tower
9: High crosses

distributed around the cathedral and a remarkable range of inscribed slabs is displayed in the adjacent visitor centre (Figs.89-90).

On the cathedral is positioned near the centre of the enclosure and there are five smaller churches clustered around it. These include Temple Connor, Temple Ciaran, Temple Melaghlin, and Temple Dowling, with Temple Finghin positioned against the outer face of the northern enclosure. Like Glendalough, most of the churches are unroofed and in ruins. There is, however, evidence that a number of other churches existed both inside and outside the enclosure. The cathedral was originally a single-chamber structure with antae, which was later modified. An extension was added to the south side and a pointed arched doorway was inserted into the west wall (Fig. 134).

On the south side of the cathedral, Temple Doolin also began as a single-chamber church with antae (Fig. 135), but it was also considerably altered during the seventeenth century a second church, Temple Hurpan was built against the east end. Near the east end of the

Fig. 134: The cathedral, Early Christian site, Clonmacnoise, County Offaly.

cathedral is Temple Ciaran. This is a small oratory-like church similar in scale to the Priest's House in Glandalough. The building has antae, but it is now in ruins (Fig. 136). Temple Finghin is one of the most unusual churches in Clonmacnoise. It has a Romanesque nave and chancel that survives only in parts. The unusual feature is the round tower that was built into the south wall (Fig. 137).

The Clonmacnoise enclosure also contains three churches that were erected in the centuries following the Early Christian period. These are Temple Melaghlin on the south east side of the cathedral, Temple Kelly on the north-east side, and Temple Connor near the northern boundary. The second and outlying enclosure in Clonmacnoise lies well to the west of the main site. Here the Nun's church, one of the finest of the Irish Romanesque churches partially survives, with only the base of the main walls and splendid Romanesque chancel arch and west doorway intact (Fig. 108).

Fig. 135: Temple Doolin, Early Christian site, Clonmacnoise, County Offaly.

Fig. 136: Temple Ciaran, Early Christian site, Clonmacnoise, County Offaly.

Fig. 137: Temple Finghin, Early Christian site, Clonmacnoise, County Offaly.

URBAN SITES

In a number of cases, the success and the development of some monasteries was so dynamic that they progressed into early forms of settlement, or towns. In many of these cases, the inner enclosure retained its religious function while the outer enclosure embraced a more secular use. At the same time the curved enclosure lines developed into roadways where they often survive in the street patterns of today. The eastern approach route continued to retain its importance and a triangular market area often developed, at a point where the approach road met the curved road line. In addition, the settlement frequently became the hub of a cluster of intersecting roads. The period during which this transition from monastery to settlement took place is uncertain, but it probably began around the tenth century. Why this process of change took place in some instances and not in others is the uncertain. Armagh, Cork, Dublin, Duleek, Galway, Kells, Kildare, Lusk, Tuam, and Wexford, for example, all emerged as successful towns, and even today their circular street patterns reflect their Early Christian origins. In contrast, the equally significant monastic sites at Clonmacnoise, Glendalough, and Monasterboice failed to achieve any level of urban form.

ARMAGH

Armagh city, in County Armagh, represents one of the most notable examples of the survival of an Early Christian layout into modern times. Here, the double circular street pattern, positioned on the crown of a steep hill, signals the centre of the present city and testifies to its Early Christian origins (Fig. 138). The original monastery dates from the fifth-century foundation by St Patrick who, it is claimed, established his principal church here. The oval-shaped inner enclosure of the original monastery is traceable in the curved course of Castle Street and Callan Street. This street line is incomplete in the northern sector, but the line of the monastic enclosure remains traceable in the property boundaries that exist in this area. The outer enclosure circuit is equally clear and is highlighted by the curve of the outer circular road, which continues from the north of the complex right

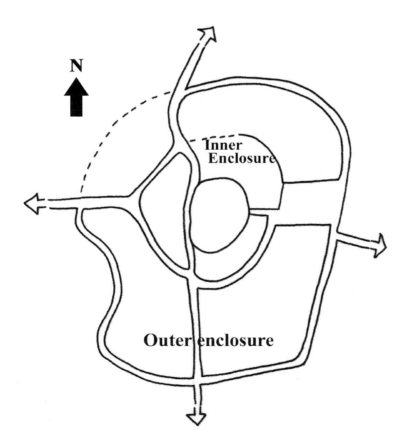

Fig. 138: Sketch layout, Armagh, County Armagh.

around to the west, with only a stretch in the north-western corner missing. The plan also highlights the sequence of roads that radiate outwards from the central core. Chief amongst these is the principal eastern approach road that enters the market place and links the inner and outer roadways. The market place is now rectangular, but in its initial form it may have been triangular. With the exception of the cemetery in the inner core, little of the monastic fabric survives, although it is known that two churches, a library, high crosses, a priory, and a round tower existed on the site.

KELLS

In a similar fashion, the town of Kells, in County Meath displays its Early Christian origins. The monastic foundation here was established in the early ninth century by a group of monks who had fled Iona, in the wake of Viking raids on the monastery there. Like Armagh, the present street pattern of the town carries the imprint of a monastic double circular plan. The rectangular inner enclosure of the monastery survives, around which winds the inner roadway on the north, east and south sides. Well beyond this the curved course of Fair Green, Carrick Street, Castle Street, and Cross Street mark the line of the outer enclosure. In addition, the main approach route to the town, John Street, is from the

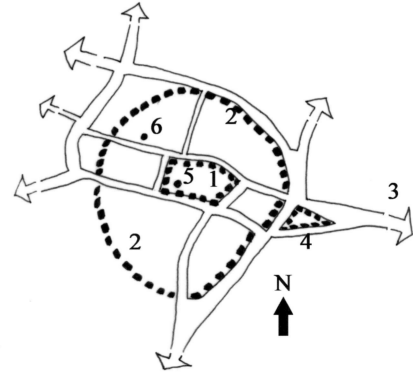

Fig: 139. Sketch layout, Kells, County Meath:
1: Inner Enclosure
2: Outer Enclosure
3: Eastern Approach Road
4: Market Place
5: Round Tower
6: St Columb's House

east and is clearly identifiable, as is the triangular market area, which has been built over in the past. Inside the inner core, the round tower and a group of stone high crosses testify to the early foundation date of the settlement (Fig.139). A most unusual survival from the Early Christian period is the small stone-roofed church, St Columb's House, which lies on the north side of Church Lane (Fig.70).

CLOSURE

The middle of the twelfth century brought a marked decline in the Early Christian monastic movement. In 1142, St Malachy, the Archbishop of Armagh, invited St Bernard to set up a Cistercian monastery in Ireland. This new community, with its new approach to religious life, was granted a site in Mellifont in County Louth by Donogh O'Carroll and fifteen years later the church was consecrated. The new monastery was laid out in conformity to a standard Cistercian plan, with a central quadrangular cloister, around which the church, administration buildings and monks' quarters were formally arranged. In addition, the Transitional Gothic style of architecture, with its large well lit churches, pointed arches, vertical emphasis and realistically inspired stone carving was introduced. The Irish Church took enthusiastically to this new monastic style and architecture, and within a century over thirty-five Cistercian houses had been established around the country. During the same period, large numbers of other European and English religious communities such as the Augustinians, Dominicans and Franciscans established Irish houses. Under this new influence the early monasteries were gradually abandoned. The Early Christian and Irish Romanesque movements had run their course and the development of the only recognisable Irish styles of architecture slowly came to a close.

TEN

GAZETTEER

This Gazetteer offers a list of sites where the visitor can find excellent examples of Ireland's Iron Age and Early Christian material. The list is a selected one, as the inclusion of all such historic sites lies outside the scope of this guide. The sites are presented on a county by county basis within their respective provinces. Those prefaced by an asterisk are discussed in detail in the main text. In addition to the site material itself, both Clonmacnoise and Glendalough have excellent visitor centres that offer a range of exhibits as well as video presentations. Furthermore, the National Heritage Park in County Wexford, the Craggaunowen crannog site in County Clare and the Navan Fort Centre in County Armagh offer examples of reconstructed domestic and religious buildings and monuments. Finally, when visiting the sites it is important to remember that many are in private ownership and permission to access must be secured from the owners. This is seldom denied, but where it is, for security or other reasons, the wishes of the owners must be respected.

ULSTER

COUNTY ANTRIM

Altagore: Stone fort.
Antrim: Round tower, bullaun stone.
Ballywee: Early Christian settlement, line of enclosure, souterrain.
Deer Park Farms: Ring-fort.
Derrykeigan: Decorated stone.
Lissue: Ring-fort.

COUNTY ARMAGH

Armagh City: Early Christian lines of enclosure.
Armagh Cathedral: Range of stone carvings, human, cult and animal figures.
Black Pig's Dyke: Linear earthworks.
Haughey's Fort: Hill fort.
Kilnasagart: Inscribed slab.
King's Stables: Ritual site.
Navan Fort: Hill fort, Visitor Centre.

COUNTY CAVAN

Black Pig's Dyke: Linear earthworks.
Drumlane: Round tower.
Killycluggin: Decorated stone (Copy).

COUNTY DERRY

Banagher: Early Christian site, church, crosses, bullaun stone.
Maghera: Early Christian site, Romanesque church.

COUNTY DONEGAL

Beltany: Carved head.
★Carndonagh: Early Christian site, cross, inscribed slabs.
Dun Lough: Stone fort.
★Grianan: Stone fort.
Tory Island: Round tower, cross, remains of churches.

COUNTY DOWN

Downpatrick: Early Christian site, line of enclosure.
Drumena: Stone fort and souterrain.
Lignagade/Lisnavaragh: Adjacent ring-forts.
★Nendrum: Early Christian site, line of triple enclosure, round tower, church.

COUNTY FERMANAGH

★Boa Island: Exceptional pre-Christian stone figures.
★Black Pig's Dyke: Linear earthworks.
Devinish: Early Christian site, round tower, bullaun stone, cross, inscribed slabs.
White Island: Early Christian site, outstanding stone figures, Romanesque church.

COUNTY MONAGHAN

★Black Pig's Dyke: Linear earthworks.
Clones: Early Christian site, high cross, round tower, church.

COUNTY TYRONE

Clogher: Hill fort, high crosses.
Errigal Keerogue: Early Christian site.
Tullaghoge: Hill fort, inauguration site.

LEINSTER

COUNTY CARLOW

St Mullins: Early Christian site, church, round tower, high cross.

COUNTY DUBLIN

Dublin City: Early Christian lines of enclosure.
★National Museum: Outstanding range of Iron Age and Early Christian elements and artefacts.
Clondalkin: Early Christian site, part of enclosure, round tower, church, high cross.
Dalkey Island: Early Christian island site, church, inscribed slabs.
★Loughshinney: Promontory fort.
Lusk: Early Christian site, line of enclosure, round tower.
Rathmichael: Early Christian site, base of round tower, Early Christian church, inscribed slabs, adjacent cross.

COUNTY KILDARE

★Castledermot: Early Christian Site, part of enclosure, Romanesque church, round tower, high crosses.
★Dun Aillinne: Hill Fort.
Kildare: Early Christian settlement, part of enclosure, round tower, high cross.
★Moone: Early Christian site, line of enclosure, high cross.
★Old Kilcullen: Early Christian site, church, round tower, high crosses.

COUNTY KILKENNY

★Freestone Hill: Hill fort.
Kilkenny City: Early Christian settlement, line of enclosure, round tower.
Kilkieran: High cross.
Kilree: Early Christian site, round tower, church, high cross.
Tullaherin: Early Christian site, round tower, church, Ogham stone.
Ullard: Early Christian site, Romanesque church, high cross.

COUNTY LAOIS

★Killeshin: Early Christian site, Romanesque church, round tower.
Timahoe: Early Christian site, round tower.

COUNTY LONGFORD

Ardagh: Early Christian church.

Corlea: Unique wooden track way.

Inchcleraun: Early Christian site, line of enclosure, churches.

COUNTY LOUTH

Drumiskin: Early Christian site, churches, round tower, high cross.

★Monasterboice: Early Christian site, line of enclosure, round tower, high crosses, inscribed slab.

★Newtownbalregan: Souterrain.

COUNTY MEATH

★Ballynee: Souterrain.

Castlekeeran: Early Christian site, church, high crosses, Ogham stone, inscribed slab.

Danestown: Ring-fort.

Duleek: Early Christian site, line of enclosure, round tower.

★Hill of Ward: Ritual site.

★Kells: Early Christian site, line of enclosure, church, round tower, high crosses.

★Tara: Exceptional hill fort site, extensive earthworks.

Telltown: Ritual site.

COUNTY OFFALY

★Clonmacnoise: Exceptional Early Christian site, round towers, churches, high crosses, Visitor Centre.

★Durrow: Early Christian site, high cross, inscribed slab.

Kinnity: High cross.

COUNTY WESTMEATH

Ushnagh: Ritual site.

Inchbofin: Early Christian site, Romanesque church, part of enclosure.

COUNTY WEXFORD

Ferns: Early Christian site, parts of dual enclosure, high cross.

Wexford Town: Early Christian site, lines of enclosure.

Ferrycarrig: Visitor Centre.

COUNTY WICKLOW

★Aghowle: Early Christian site, line of enclosure, Romanesque church, high cross, bullaun stone.

★Wicklow Complex: Extensive hill fort complex.

★Glendalough: Early Christian Site, part of enclosure, cathedral, Romanesque churches, churches, round tower, stone fort, high cross, bullaun stones, inscribed slabs, Visitor Centre.

Rathgall: Hill fort.
Tuckmil Upper: Hill fort.

MUNSTER

COUNTY CLARE

Ballykinvara: Stone fort.
Beal Boru: Ring-fort.
Cahercommoun: Complex stone fort.
Cathermacnaughten: Stone fort, huts.
Corrofin: Stone fort.
Dysert O'Dea: Early Christian site, part of enclosure, round tower, church, high cross, inscribed slabs.
Inishcaltra: Early Christian island site, part of enclosure, round tower churches, hut, cross.
Kilfenora: Early Christian site, churches, crosses.
Killaloe: Romanesque churches, high cross.
Magh Adhair: Inauguration site.
Mooghaun: Hill fort.
Scattery: Early Christian island site, round tower, cathedral, Romanesque church, inscribed slab.
Craggaunowen:Visitor Centre

COUNTY CORK

Ballycrovane: Particularly tall Ogham stone.
Black Ditch: Linear earthworks.
Cashel: Hill fort.
Carn Tigherna: Hill fort.
Knockdrum: Stone fort, souterrain.
Garranes: Ring-fort.
Kinneigh: Early Christian site, unusual round tower with hexagonal base.
Labbamolaga: Early Christian site, part of enclosure, churches.

COUNTY KERRY

Aghadoe: Early Christian site, round tower, Romanesque church, Ogham stone.
Ardfert: Early Christian site, Romanesque cathedral, Romanesque church.
Beebane: Stone fort, souterrain, hut.
Cahergall: Stone fort, huts.
Cloughanecarhan: Ringfort, beehive hut, Ogham stone.
Dingle: Unparallel range of exceptional early Christian sites with enclosures, Romanesque churches, early churches, Ogham stones, inscribed stones, souterrains, stone forts, promontory forts.

Dunbeg: Promontory fort.

★*Illauntannig Island*: Early Christian site, line of enclosure with wall chamber, beehive huts, church.

Inisfallen: Early Christian site, Romanesque church.

★*Kilmalkedar*: Romanesque church.

★*Leacanabuaile*: Stone fort, hut, souterrain.

Ratass: Early Christian site, church, Ogham stone, inscribed slab.

★*Skellig Michael*: Exceptional Early Christian island site, part of enclosure, beehive huts, churches, inscribed slabs.

★*Staigue*: Stone fort.

COUNTY LIMERICK

Ardagh: Ring-fort.

Ardpatrick: Early Christian site, part of enclosure. round tower, church.

Ballylin: Hill fort.

Lough Gur: Complex Early Christian site, ring-forts, stone forts.

Mungret: Early Christian site, churches.

Red Ditch: Linear earthworks.

COUNTY TIPPERARY

Aheny: High cross.

★*Ballycrine*: Ring-fort.

★*Cashel*: Early Christian site, part of enclosure, Romanesque church, high crosses, round tower.

Liathmore: Early Christian site, churches, round tower.

★*Lorrah*: Early Christian sites, part of enclosure, church, high cross.

Monaincha: Early Christian site, high cross.

★*Rathurlas*: Ring-fort.

★*Roscrea*: Early Christian site, part of enclosure, round tower, Romanesque church, high cross.

COUNTY WATERFORD

★*Ardmore*: Early Christian site, Romanesque church, round tower, Ogham stone.

Black Ditch: Linear earthworks.

★*Drumlohan*: Ogham stones, souterrain.

CONNAUGHT

COUNTY GALWAY

★*Aughrim*: Ring-fort

Aran Islands: Exceptional and extensive range of Early Christian sites, churches, stone huts, crosses, round towers, inscribed slabs. Also extensive range of ring-forts, stone forts and promontory forts.

Dun Aonghasa: Spectacular stone fort.

Turoe: Exceptional carved stone with adjoining ring-fort.

Clonfert: Romanesque church.

High Island: Early Christian site, church, stone huts, inscribed slabs.

Inchagoill: Early Christian site, Romanesque church, inscribe slabs.

Kilbennan: Ruins of Romanesque church and round tower.

Kilmacduagh: Early Christian site, round tower, cathedral, churches.

Roscam: Early Church site, part of enclosure, round tower.

St MacDara: Early Christian island site, church.

Tuam: Early Christian site, part of enclosure, high cross.

COUNTY MAYO

Inishglora: Early Christian site, part of enclosure, churches, huts, inscribed slabs.

Inishkea: Early Christian island site, church, huts, inscribed slabs.

Killala: Early Christian settlement, round tower.

COUNTY ROSCOMMON

Castlestrange: Decorated stone.

Rathcrughan: Extensive and complex ritual site.

COUNTY SLIGO

Clogher: Stone fort, souterrains.

Drumcliff: Early Christian site, round tower, high cross.

Inismurray: Early Christian site, line of enclosure, churches, crosses, huts, inscribed slabs.